# COVID-19

## CHINA'S GIFT

### TO THE WORLD

CHAPLAIN ZACHARY H.F.

**Disclaimer:**

Articles referenced are used under the 'Doctrine of Fair Use' for educational purposes only!

The annotated articles include new information concerning the origins of COVID-19 *and* it is also a summation of a multitude of information concerning the Coronavirus that has claimed over One Million lives worldwide...*and counting!* It is intended to educate the public with information compiled from sources you may not be aware of.

Permission Granted: *War on the Rocks*, Ryan Evens, Texas National Security Review, email dtd: 29 October 20.

Permission Granted: *Agenda 2030*, Todd Hampson.

Permission Granted: *Now The End Begins*, by Geoffery Grider.

Permission Granted: Ron Paul Institute (on article website).

Permission Granted: *Rapture Ready*, Diamond Duck

I can be contacted at: writingainteasy@gmail.com

Website: VictorGraphics.com

www.covid19chinasgifttotheworld.com

Cover by: pro_ebookcovers@fiveer.com

Professional Editing Software: ProWritingAid

Library of Congress Number: TXu00222095

Paperback ISBN: 978-0-9997931-5-2

eBook ISBN: 978-0-9997931-4-5

# Acknowledgments

*Dedicated to the Holy Trinity with whom 'All Things' are possible!*

***In loving memory of***
Lillian "Grandmother" Johnson-Gains
(1905-1996)

**Dedicated to my Grandfather's in the Ministry:**

Dr. J. Vernon McGee     Thru The Bible Radio
ttb.org

Pastor Chuck Smith      Calvary Chapel Costa Mesa
Twft.com

Dr. Adrian Rodgers      Bellevue Baptist Church
Lwf.org

**Dedicated to my Father in the Ministry:**

Dr. France A. Davis     Calvary Baptist Church, Salt Lake
Calvaryslc.com          City, Utah

**My Pastor:**

Carlos 'Charlie' Flores     Calvaryep.com

# Table of Contents

## CHAPTER 1

# COVID-19: China's Gift to the World

## China's Crisis, China's Opportunity

*China cannot intentionally initiate a pandemic that would cause the world goes to war against them as this would crush the world dominance that China is trying to achieve, however…it does not mean that they did not set loose the virus on the world.*

- Chaplain Zachary

### What the Hell Happened?

I am just the average American like you are and seeking answers just like the journalists we see on the major news networks and newspapers. As a concerned citizen, I know we must not just know how this COVID-19 virus is affecting us as Americans, but we must also see this from the eyes of China. I have two master's degrees, and I am a Board-Certified Chaplain, but neither of these accomplishments has anything to do with China or this virus.

1

This is the third Flu virus to come from China and naturally, they have plenty of experience on how to contain it. It is very clear that China has progressed from containment to now using viruses to its advantage while the rest of the world, with very little pandemic exposure, attempt to recover from its economic collapse and reopening slowly while China has reopened its economy and we're buying a multitude of consumer goods from them.

An article by Bangladesh News, featuring Steven Lee Myers and Chris Buckley of the NYT, reference President Xi Jinping himself acknowledging China's time has arrived:[1]

As we seen on the major news networks, in the six days after top Chinese officials secretly determined they likely were facing a pandemic from a new coronavirus, the city of Wuhan at the epicenter of the disease, hosted a mass banquet for tens of thousands of people for Lunar New Year celebrations.

As we have learned, China suppressed data and changed data. Samples were destroyed, contaminated areas scrubbed, and early reports of the virus by Chinese virologists was erased. We also heard on the news that doctors and journalists in China who were sounding the alarm *disappeared*. They were warning of the spread of the virus and its contagious nature from human to human, yet China silenced them and

---

[1] https://bdnews24.com/world/asia-pacific/2020/05/21/in-chinas-crisis-xi-sees-a-crucible-to-strengthen-his-rule.

moved quickly to shut down travel domestically from Wuhan to the rest of China but did not stop international flights from Wuhan to the four corners of the world.

This is the essence of Communism, a means to completely control the actions of others. China sought to control the WHO (World Health Organization) dissemination of information concerning the origins of the virus and how contagious the virus really was. All of this in an attempt to deflect China's role in this worldwide pandemic. The world now sees through China's lies and true motives. China has sought to bully all nation that attributes the origin of the Coronavirus to them with treats of tariffs and other economic sanctions.

How could we (the world) have been deceived for so long as to the true intentions of China? Under the NAFTA agreement, We sent factories to them for cheap labor and now the chickens have come home to roost. We have learned that China makes and controls much of the essential lifesaving drugs we depend on every day and threatened to withhold shipment of these items if America did not stop blaming China for the origins of the Coronavirus.

It's like, 'who have I been in bed with all of these years'! Like, when you think you know someone, and their true character is revealed years later and now you're somewhat stuck in a bad relationship. Well, our eyes are wide open now, and America, as well as many other nations, are in the process of getting…unstuck.

CHAPTER 2

# China's Playbook for World Domination

## A History of China's Proven Strategies with Pandemics

After researching and much reading, I came across this article below, it is clear to me that China intended to use this COVID-19 pandemic to replace America as the number one economy in the world. This article is *damming* in the worst way and should be a wake-up call to the WORLD! This article is by Diana Fu, she is associate professor of political sciences at The University of Toronto and an affiliate of the Munk School of Global Affairs and Public Policy Asian Institute. Her research examines popular contention, state power, civil society, and citizenship, with a focus on contemporary China. The article is entitled "China Has a Playbook for Managing Coronavirus Chaos." Convincing the world that freedom is worth it will be a hard struggle if Beijing sells its message right.[2]

In her article, she seeks to inform governments around the world that the underlying threat of the current pandemic is

---

[2] https://foreignpolicy.com/2020/05/05/china-coronavirus-chaos-playbook-stability/

not just death, but chaos. Out of chaos there must be order. She concludes the mandate of all governments is to seek the opposite of chaos and maintaining order. The conclusion of her article addresses the current competition between democratic societies in the West and authoritarian regimes such as China is about who can restore political order quickly and at what cost.

After reading her article, I have a better view of the Chinese Communist mentality which overwhelmingly concludes that China will never play by the rules of a free society. The same can be said for North Korea and most of Islam. Though not a Communist regime, Russia and Iran also have ambition of world dominance. In war, America would be doing the same thing China is doing to topple China, but we are not at war, in fact, had China just been honest from the beginning, they very well could have been the darling of the nations. If they were willing to share information and PPE (Personal Protective Equipment), the entire world would be on a path to recovery sooner that we are now–eleven months later. But instead, China seen the opportunity to share the virus with the world and hoped to make their debut as a leader in the fight against infectious diseases.

There is a book that outlines China's strategy for world dominance and reviewed by our military and we can clearly see China abiding by its well documented strategy. The title of the book is '*Unrestrictive Warfare.*' It details how to win a *cold war* with technology and placing Chinese loyalists in strategic positions in nations around the world:[3]

**Précis: Unrestricted Warfare**

"In 1999, Chinese People's Liberation Army Cols. Qiao Liang and Wang Xiangsui published what would prove to be a highly influential book titled Unrestricted Warfare. The authors argued that modern war at that time had evolved past using only armed forces "to compel the enemy to submit to one's will" into using all military and nonmilitary means to compel an enemy to capitulate to a state's political objectives. According to their analysis, in the modern, highly competitive, globalized world, the roles of soldiers and civilians had been fundamentally erased because the equivalent of war among states in the modern world would now be ongoing continuously and everywhere.

The authors go on to postulate tactics for developing countries to use against more technologically advanced nations in the event of an overt outbreak of hostilities, implying that such measures should be used to chart the course China had to take to compensate for its then military inferiority to the United States. They outline the synchronized employment of a multitude of means to be used concurrently with military force to prevail in a conflict including hacking into government websites underpinning an opponent's

---

[3] https://warontherocks.com/2016/04/a-new-generation-of-unrestricted-warfare/

administration of government, disrupting financial institutions, exploiting the West's open media, promoting social discord, and conducting urban warfare.

In a separate interview translated by the U.S. Foreign Broadcast Information Service (FBIS), Qiao was quoted as stating that "the first rule of unrestricted warfare is that there are no rules, with nothing forbidden."

The authors' contentions foreshadowed not only the direction of Chinese development across the spectrum of its elements of national power but may have been the origin of more recent similar assertions by modern Russian military theorists. As a result, any serious student of modern warfare would be well advised to become acquainted with this influential work.

There are various commercial translations available of Unrestricted Warfare. However, Military Review recommends an abridged version derived from a translation by FBIS available at https://www.c4i.org/unrestricted.pdf. For those interested in more detail, the background and significance of Unrestricted Warfare on modern military thought, we invite you to read "A New Generation of Unrestricted Warfare," by retired Lt. Gen. David W. Barno and Dr. Nora Bensahel, published in War on the Rocks on 19 April 2016."

## Proof

China's Thousand Talent Program is proof of their *cold war* infiltration of nations. Officials are concerned about spying and intellectual-property theft. This was aired by all of the major news media. The report stated that China was using a wide range of methods to export American technology. You, like I, probably had never heard of the Thousand Talent Program. As I understand it, they got agreements with the heads of universities here in America to operate on their campuses, under Chinese law, for large sums of money. That particular media story I watched on Fox News.[4] What seemed like a good partnership with China to exchange knowledge and technology turned out to be foreign espionage.

It is public knowledge that China, Russia, Iran, and North Korea has been relentlessly hacking into American technology companies to steal Top Secret and other sensitive data to compete with America. This is more evident in the race to develop a cure for the Coronavirus. The article concluded that, "The economic and strategic losses for the United States are increasingly unsustainable, threatening not only to help China gain global dominance of a number of the leading technologies of the future, but also to undermine America's commercial and military advantages."

---

[4] https://www.foxnews.com/tech/china-is-using-economic-espionage-and-theft-to-grab-us-technology.

What's frightening to me is that so much of what we're hearing in the news on the major news networks would have continued as normal had it not been for the Coronavirus becoming a worldwide pandemic and China's coverup of the origins and timing of the spread of the virus. The entire world is demanding answers, yet China still continues to maintain their innocence of the origins of the Coronavirus. I, for one, am personally grateful that President Trump is holding China accountable for the origin and spread of COVID-19.

CHAPTER 3

# Why is the World Still Guessing?

On Tucker Carlson Tonight, Fox News, dtd 27 October 2020, the question was asked by Alex Berensen, 'Why do we still not know where the Coronavirus originated'?[5] In that article, he called for an international investigation of into the origins of COVID-19. This is something, in my opinion, should have been initiated at the U.N. (United Nations). It should have been investigated months ago. It just goes to show how deeply rooted China is in world affairs.

In the pay for play' scheme, China has done a brilliant job during this cold war in controlling high level executives of very powerful organizations and nations to force their will on the world. All the while, the rest of the world, members of the U.N., are playing by rules for honest and fair trade. In that article, Mr. Berensen also mentioned scientists had been conducting what is known as "gain of function research" at the Wuhan Institute of Virology. He goes on to state that the process involves manipulating a virus to make it more virulent in order to identify "what natural virus might become dangerous to humans if it mutated in various ways."

---

[5]https://www.foxnews.com/media/alex-berenson-coronavirus-wuhan-lab-china.

## Is COVID-19 a Man-made Bioweapon?

I firmly believe so! Dr. Ai Fen, a Chinese Virologist, went missing a week after she first reported on the virus in China. I have seen and read the article and invite you to do so too.[6] She was the head of Emergency at Wuhan Central Hospital. Why would China detain her is China had nothing to hide? Why was her interview taken down off of China's People magazine website and her picture removed? Common sense say China is clearly covering their tracks.

My person of interest whom I believe offer the most compelling evidence of the Coronavirus originating in Wuhan China is Dr. Li-Meng Yan. I first encountered her story on Tucker Carlson Tonight, Fox News.[7] She is 100% convinced that the virus was intentionally created in a Chinese lab. She stated she worked in the WHO Reference Lab, which she states is the top coronavirus lab in the world. She now has 'whistleblower' status here in the U.S.

During that interview, she stated that she believed China intentionally released the virus. Why would she lie? Why would she risk being deported by China (though America will not allow that to happen) to be silenced or made to disappear? On another segment, she stated that her mother had been

---

[6] https://www.rfa.org/english/news/china/concerns-03302020150737.html.

[7] https://www.oann.com/virologist-says-there-is-evidence-covid-19-was-man-made-in-wuhan/

detained by the Chinese government because of her exposing China as being totally at fault for this worldwide pandemic.

Why wouldn't we believer her? She's an insider. She was a wealthy doctor, why would she risk all of that for a lie? I believe, as she said, that the Chinese government intentionally manufactured and released COVID-19 on the world. If we remember, after only about two or three months, China celebrated the Chinese Lunar New Year in Wuhan just to prove to the world that they contained the virus. This indeed made them seem like they were very proficient in handling contagious diseases. However, no one was allowed in to inspect the true conditions of Wuhan and the effects the virus was having on their people.

Were all of the residents at the festival actually residents of Wuhan or some other providence where the virus had not arrived and they were brought there for show. We will never know because of the power of the Chinese government to lock its borders and censor its people.

In Yan's comments, she conflicted with the opinion of Dr. Anthony Fauci, director of the National Institute of Allergy and Infectious Diseases and White House coronavirus adviser, who previously cast doubt on the idea the virus was artificially created. The world was already very angry at China for hiding the initial outbreak of the virus and covering their tracks, even to the point of influencing the president of

WHO to refrain from sounding the alarm to the world. I am very happy that President Trump held the president of WHO accountable for catering to China. Through all of the initial spread of the virus, China's mask is off and they are now exposed as an evil tyrant lusting for world domination.

With the evidence I have read and presented to you, of which you can check out for yourself, is clear proof that China manufactured this virus as a means of toppling America as the top super power.

## What Great Leverage Does China have on the U.S.?

What great leverage China has is influenced by their supply chain over the US. In May 2020, Congress spent $3T on a Coronavirus Relief Bill. And with that money, we have to continue to buy essential goods and lifesaving medicine from China. China knew this. That is one reason why they quietly purchased billions of dollars' worth of PPE to sell to nations around the world at inflated prices.

What China has done is caused an artificial inflation on all affected nations with the Coronavirus. We are emergency spending to keep the economy afloat, yet the massive layoffs of workers because of the fear of the unknown, is fueling inflation at a rapid pace and who stands to gain the most...China! I am quite sure that only America is going to hold China accountable because of the strong leadership in the Trump Administration. Why do I say this, because previous presidents hasn't held China accountable for the trade deficit until the Trump Administration. We are also learning that China has been filling the pockets of politicians, both Democrat and Republican. If President Trump had been a career politician, China would surely be shining brighter than the U.S. as the new world economic leader.

I have learned that in the pecking order of U.S. debt, China is far down on the list of America's I.O.U., Japan is the biggest national foreign holder of American debt, followed by American investors in American Bonds, followed by the Federal Reserve, and then China.

## CHAPTER 4

# Proactive vs Reactive

**The Asian Wet Markets are still selling bats and monkeys.**

The bat that host this virus was 800 miles away in a cave where it was caught and brought to the Level P4 Weapons lab. There are no coincidences in China. The ground-zero patient in Wuhan was within yards of that P4 Lab. The bats that are consumed in the wet markets are not the same bats that spawned this virus. The bat that matches the genetic code of the Coronavirus is 800 miles away in the caves that the bat lady went to in order to bring viruses back for the P4 Weapons Lab to study.[8]

Each pandemic has had a 'reactive' effect and understandably so. Technology to detect diseases and viruses just was not available. The most scientists can do is reverse engineer a newly discovered virus. In the midst of the COVID-19 pandemic, we are in a position to be proactive from this point forward. If 'wet' markets are not going away, which the average person can rightly conclude it will not because of the almighty dollar–no matter what currency, demand will

---

[8] https://www.foxnews.com/shows/justice-jeanine

not allow it to close. The only other option is weekly random testing. Ideally, a *test group* of local volunteers must be created and weekly monitored. We have seen how a virus can lay undetected for a week before symptoms appear. A test group will prevent the need for a *black market* to provide exotic animals in high demand by the wealthy. This would be similar to America legalizing marijuana in hopes of combating the illegal sale of the drug and, of course, taking what would have been solely drug cartel money and legally adding it to the treasury. The wild exotic animals sold in wet markets are a delicacy mostly enjoyed by the wealthy.

A test group of people who live near a wet market like the Wuhan wet market in China, where the virus escaped, need to be in a controlled community, perhaps with its own school so that the children do not come in contact with other children. This controlled community will live their lives as usual with their blood samples taken weekly. There must be normal daily interaction with visitors to the wet markets with the controlled community allowed shop normally and buy the items they regularly eat. The wet market would not be cleaned any more than normal to mimic a normal daily shopping environment. The people of the controlled environment would shop as normal, whether they be shopping for a holiday, birthday, or an anniversary where a loved one's favorite food is purchased. Whatever is one the menu in public view or special ordered, the controlled group must have access to...*including* the exotic animals the wealthy have access to.

Weekly, they must be tested and screened for any virus. This would then send the world into lockdown mode if a virus is detected. From the Coronavirus and well into the future, lockdown procedures should be in place, especially at airports. Just as importantly, boarders where illegal immigrants may enter must be closed. America stopped flights from China, but they entered through other porous openings into America. The wearing of masks and social distancing must be implemented immediately when out in public...and enforced with a curfew by all policing agents available to each state. Not a total lockdown. The precedence has been set, war has been declared, clear offensive objectives has been established, and must be carried out as in any war. The enemy is invisible to the human eye, deadly, and determined to survive. Any *civilian* soldier not carrying out their orders would be committing treason and worthy of catching the virus.

Stockpiles of PPE (Personnel Protective Equipment) must be readily on hand as well as known vaccination medicines, even though a new strand of virus has many unknowns. COVID-19 has many of unknowns, yet Chloroquine and Hydroxychloroquine, anti-malarial drugs, have had some positive effects against COVID-19 and something is *better* than nothing. Having *something* gives hope as daily news briefings from top government officials and medical experts gives encouragement and hope. It is way too late to be blaming current or past Administrations, though the CDC should have helped America be more responsive. I will acknowledge that the current Trump administration had increased funding to the CDC as this is simply a matter of public record. I am neither endorsing nor condemning either party because under President W. George Bush *and* President Barrack Obama *both* failed to adequately prepare America.

Until there is a cure for the Coronavirus, this is how I believe we move forward. In studying the Spanish Flu of 1918, it was a year before the pandemic ended with about 50 million people dead because of it. It is a hope and a prayer that the Coronavirus will end in the coming summer months. If so, we will have frantically implemented measures that we should have learned from the H1N1 virus as well as the H5N1 virus.

## CHAPTER 5

# Globalist Agenda

Many of us are hearing about the Globalist Agenda for the first time. It has been in the making for a long time at the UN (United Nations).

Up front. For the globalist agenda to become a reality, a *free enterprise* economy *'must'* go away for a globalist government to exist. In addition, every person must have a RFID (Radio Frequency Identification) or some type of 'mark' to track their every step. After ID tagging each citizen, then you can now control them. The COVID-19 is an excellent opportunity for Globalist to make great strides in their global agenda. It has to be a big enough crisis to crash the economy where we look for a permanent solution to a worldwide pandemic such as COVID-19. I have no doubt in my mind, the world's reaction to COVID-19 is being studied in great detail which will produce a 'master plan' for the next *manmade* pandemic.

**America's Fiat Currency**

COVID-19 exposed just how fragile the world economy is. In 1944, the US Dollar was chosen as the world's currency.

Rather than using gold as a means of exchange, as was the world's standard, the dollar was chosen because back then, the American dollar was as good as gold. Under this new system, countries agreed to fix their currency to the US Dollar. This meant countries around the world could exchange their currency for US dollars. The US dollar would be tied to the price of gold at $35 dollars an ounce at that time. This created a system where all currencies were essentially backed by gold. To avoid the logistics of shipping physical gold around the world, it was stored safely here in America.

The problem began when America began to run budget deficits. We were fighting the war in Vietnam and we were running the Great Society program under President Lyndon B. Johnson. With all the spending in the US, other countries could see that America was running a deficit and became concerned and began demanding gold for their US dollars instead of Federal Reserve Notes. They felt that there were more dollars being printed than gold that backed it. To prevent this outflow of gold from American vaults, in August 1971, President Richard Nixon called for an emergency suspension of the Gold Convertibility System. He took action by directing the Secretary of Finance to take the necessary action to defend the dollar against speculators. He suspended the convertibility of gold or other Reserve assets.

All of the monetary deficits experienced today by the Federal Government stems from that August 15th decision by

President Nixon by abandoning the fixed link back to gold. What gold did was providing spending discipline in governments where you spent only up to the amount you had. Under the old system, if America ran a deficit, gold would flow out of the country until there was a balance again by paying off the deficit. Without gold backing, not only did America run a deficit, but so did the countries that traded with the US dollar. The Dollar now only becomes as good as the American economy. America has since that time…good or bad…always ran a deficit until this very day.

The conditions that led President Nixon to abandon the gold standard were supposed to be temporary. It has now been 49 years and America is Trillions of dollars in debt! By removing the link between gold and the US dollar, President Nixon created a system where Federal Notes were backed by – 'nothing'! Yes…nothing!

The American currency system we and the world now live with is called a Fiat System. A Fiat System is a currency that is backed only by government promises…I Owe You! Fiat is a Latin word that basically means – circulating by force. If people have confidence in their currency and their government, that confidence causes the currency to circulate. Thus, when there is a market crash, the government 'must' stimulate the economy to build consumer confidence.

There is no nation on the planet that uses money (gold), we all use currency. Money is a medium of exchange and the way that it has evolved is that it is 'always' something of intrinsic value. With the link cut between the American Dollar and gold, all we supposedly need now is what we are seeing in Federal Government, which is Political Decree! Politicians have now determined that America doesn't need anything of intrinsic value. The actual dollar bill is 'decreed' money with no gold backing. Now money has a new characteristic, but underneath it all, there's the same concept in place that nobody ever seems to challenge, and that is that the American government have a right to declare something of 'no' value (US Dollar) and we must accept it."

If America is destroyed, as Muslims flew planes into the World Trade Center and tried to bomb it, as well as the Pentagon and we know they aimed for the White House, so shall all of the other world economies who trade with the US Dollar be destroyed. Thus, we see an 'intrinsic' value of an American Nation governed by godly Christian Politicians, the Ten Commandments, and the Holy Bible.

With currencies no longer backed by something of intrinsic value (gold), countries with a weak currency can make products cheaply. Countries devalue their own currency to make them a desirable trading partner. Every paper currency measures itself against the dollar. So, if the US dollar value decreases, then Central Banks around the world responds to it. They are just trying to intervene so that the impact of a decreased in value American dollar does not impact their economy.

## Global Vaccine

Another very important detail for the globalist agenda is for the vaccine to be already created and it will be the incentive for the world getting tagged. A vast majority of the population who contracted the Coronavirus has recovered. There must be a virus worse than COVID-19, or Smallpox, or Ebola to guarantee cooperation in exchange for saving one's life. A vaccine patented and controlled by China or the WHO.

The Coronavirus did spread rapidly around the world and kill a large number of people, though mostly the elderly, with a fatality rate of 3.4% as compared to the traditional yearly flu of 0.1%. in other words, a person has a 34% greater chance of dying from the Coronavirus vs the traditional flu. It clearly shut down whole economies around the world simultaneously…as if planned. If it was planned, and I do not believe it was, it would have been planned at the global level. In the race for a cure for COVID-19, the globalist agenda can still come to pass, but with a 'lot' of push back.

Rahm Emanuel, "You never let a serious crisis go to waste."

It doesn't take a lot of people to control the masses if they are at the top of an organization such as Media, Secretary of State, Supreme Court Justices.

The global vaccine agenda would cause a person to be 'tagged' and eventually...*controlled*. The vaccine is just the excuse needed to tag while the real agenda lay hidden like a virus.

If I was tagged and I started a boycott of...say...getting vaccinated against an unproven experimental drug...they would simply deactivate my RFID/Mark and I could not buy or sell and if I had $8,000 in the bank, with the use of a keyboard they would simply reduce my $8,000 to $8.00 and now I am no longer interested in boycotting, I got to try and find out why I can't purchase anything or pay my bills. That is the reality of the world being issued RFID credit cards and world tagging.

They have facial recognition software, but it would be so much easier to know if I attended a KKK rally or a Black Panther rally or a Muslim secret Mosque meeting.

They would know the time I arrived, the time I left, and who was at the meeting. They would also turn on the mic of your cell phone without your knowledge and it never left your pocket or purse. Communist countries like Russia, China, North Korea already do this with their citizens knowing and if they did not know, there is nothing they could do about it.

It is just a matter of time before elected officials who want to stay in power steer America to become the same as a Communist or Totalitarian nation. The good news is that illegal immigrants would be required to be tagged; and again, COVID-19 is a great excuse to initiate tagging at the U.N. (United Nations) level and a weak American President would go along with the program. Once tagged, then no one can buy or sell without being tagged.

Even worse than that, here in America people were actually going door to door to scan addresses in every community. This you would think seems harmless when you can type in an address and get a view of the house, but a GPS address would allow for a direct hit on a house that...*say*...where an international wanted terrorist was visiting. It would be a precise target of destruction depending on the explosives used.

We have explosives that will only destroy everything in someone's living room. A drone would simply shoot its explosive device into the living room window/bedroom windows and destroy everything/everyone inside without damaging the neighbor's homes. No need to send SWAT if they wanted everyone in the house dead. Even if a 'most wanted' criminal was traveling on a highway, he/she could be blown up by a drone right here in America if they see no cars around it. Afterwards would simply be a matter of repairing the road.

These are just some of the globalist agenda scenarios I can think of, but...to simply log into your bank account and change $8,000 to $8.00 is scary enough for me. If you haven't watched videos of military drones destroying moving vehicles and other structures on the news...you should!

It is only because of the Constitution of the U.S. that we are not a socialist nation. If you didn't know, a socialist/totalitarian nation is run like a communist nation, *but* we get to vote as long as the U.S. Constitution isn't severely amended through the political system. America is most assuredly headed towards a Socialist/Totalitarian government once a political group has determined to keep power at all costs! As we know, with Senator Bernie Sanders, America was on a straight path to socialism. Not only that, Joe Biden is piggybacking off his socialist ideas. These are facts...I am not promoting one party over another.

Social Media is controlling the voice of conservatives. Anything negative about Abortion, LGBTQ+ and Muslims...etc., is all the reason they need to censor your account, which in turn promotes their values and, at the moment, nothing can be done about it. Detailed profiles are being created for each and every one of us by social media and the government every time we log onto a computer or use our smart phone. Our personal information has been compiled by the NSA (National Security Agency) since 9/11, along with Google, Microsoft and Facebook.

Websites has been using *'cookies'* for a very long time to track our shopping, browsing, and spending habits. Because of rapid advancements in computer technology, it is estimated that knowledge is doubling every year. In his 1982 book, Critical Path, futurist and inventor R. Buckminster Fuller estimated that up until the 1900s, human knowledge doubled approximately every century. By 1945, it was doubling every 25 years and by

1982, it was doubling every 12-13 months. IBM estimated that in 2020 human knowledge will be doubling every 12 hours.[9]

## UN Agenda 21

U.N. Agenda 21 *covertly* calls for the reduction of the population by 85%. How it will do that is not known. We see the power of the Coronavirus to reduce the population, but nothing like the Spanish Flu that killed 50 Million people. I perceive reduction will start with the poorest of the poor in slums in India, Africa, the Philippines and other nations…it is quite possible they will *intentionally* send a virus by

---

[9] https://www.modernworkplacelearning.com/cild/mwl/about/

mosquitoes or other means into those populations and simply turn their backs on their cries or at least until a worldwide outcry demand their intervention. As Americans, the autonomy we have today is because of our US Constitution that guarantees certain inalienable rights as compared to the UN Constitution:

**Constitution of the United States:**

1) Our freedom comes from God

2) They cannot be numbered (freedom of speech, own property, gun, etc.)

3) They are inalienable for all men are created equal

4) They ensure religious freedom

**United Nations Constitution:**

1) Freedom *does not* come from God but Government

2) People can be numbered

3) A person's rights *can be* taken away for bad behavior

So, we see how blessed we have been as an American nation. However, we're on track for all of this to change in the very near future or with the next worldwide pandemic. Since COVID-19, proposals for a universal income, tracking ID, a cashless society, government surveillance, marginalizing the church, and much more, reveals things are falling into place for a global society.

Before the Housing Market crash of 2008, authorities kept interest rates very low in order to make money. They made money very easy to borrow. Wall Street and Politicians had agreed to work together. Wall Street for the pursuit of profits and Politicians (Clinton to present) for the pursuit of government interference on economic growth, which would result in election victories for years to come. This was the beginning of the Housing Bubble. When the bubble was expanding, everybody make money.

Banks created the Ninja loan…*no* income *no* job and *no* assets. It allowed banks to grow enormously by putting assets in the hands of tens of millions of people who couldn't afford it and selling those loans to investors around the world as securities. These Ninja loans were overwhelmingly demographically targeted to mostly Black, Latinos, the Elderly and other poor ethnic groups. We can easily see how an economy can collapse by a worldwide virus and by an orchestrated collapse of the world financial institutions like Wall Street.

CHAPTER 6

# Global Currency

### Cryptocurrency to Replace Fiat Currency

The world is fast approaching a cashless society. Bitcoin is proving that it is not only possible, but 'a matter of fact' that banks can be eliminated. Bitcoin is a straight transaction between two parties–no middleman (banks). The only reason more and more people are not using Bitcoin is because of a lack of knowledge. There is only one very real drawback to using Bitcoin and that is the encrypted 'key' the party receives. Say I send you $100,000 by Bitcoin, the government doesn't know about it, banks don't know about it, just the receiving party and I. You see, the middleman is completely eliminated; thus, no taxes or interest paid. If it sounds to good to be true–it's not and operating very well around the world. However, if you lose the encrypted 'key'…you have lost the $100,000. That's the only danger to Bitcoin. You are 100% responsible for your losses if you lose your encrypted key. But you have a considerable more amount of money in your pocket if you do not lose your encrypted key. No banking fees, no charge card fees, no taxes, just you are 100% responsible for your encrypted key.

Well, guess what? Governments are scrambling to counter Bitcoin so that they can trace every encrypted transaction. The globalist agenda will not only tract if you're vaccinated or not, your exact position on the earth, but also control of your spending if you go against government. In order for America to survive this, it must be solvent. It must not be dependent on China for most of its goods and medicine as it is now, nor any other nation. We must

have a vast amount of gold on hand as cash will soon disappear. Problem is, we're about $24 Trillion dollars in the hole! COVID-19 has caused a *free-fall* of trillion-dollar spending that we would not have been able to borrow had we not had the soaring economy we had under President Trump's administration. What's the chance of our next President standing up to China as the current administration is doing...slim to none! Therefore, the globalist agenda is knocking on America's door.

I would like to share with you some compelling information compiled by my prophecy watch friend Todd Hampson:[10]

**Agenda 2030**

"This UN manifesto of sorts was ratified and adopted on September 25, 2015. It calls for (and has been forcefully

---

[10] http://toddhampson.com/id2020-agenda2030/

moving toward) radical plans that will affect everything by the year 2030. Of course it sounds fluffy and nice, but If you read between the lines (and if you understand human nature and the God-less foundations of the UN) you'll see that it is the culmination of a decades long push toward a Global Government and a New World Order. This is not a hidden agenda. It is out in the open. Many globalists over the past 10-20 years (and longer) have openly, publicly used those specific terms. Again, take some time to research this for yourself if it sounds far-fetched. Here's the 2030 website to begin your research: https://sustainabledevelopment.un.org/post2015/transformingourworld.

## ID2020

Bill and Melinda Gates pledged $10 billion in a call for a decade of vaccines. That is the title of a press release from the Bill & Melinda Gates foundation website. So, what's wrong with that? If you're like me you have always known Bill Gates as the Microsoft computer genius who competed head-to-head with Steve Jobs and Apple. Bill is a globalist. His dad was a globalist. Again, vet what I am saying.

Last year Bill stepped down from Microsoft to pursue his new initiatives-among them ID2020 that seeks to give everyone on the planet a digital ID, and vaccinations. Neither of those are evil in themselves, but when you look at the big picture, the worldview of the players, and what the Bible says will definitely happen in the future tribulation period- everything is lining up.

So, let me connect a few dots. Bill Gates (a computer entrepreneur) has been heavily involved with the UN and the W.H.O. (the global health arm of the UN) for quite some time. The UN officially adopts a plan to change everything by 2030 with the promise that "no one will be left behind." Bill Gates pledges a "decade of vaccines" that culminates in the year 2030, and a the same time funds ID2020 with a manifesto that says (among many other things), "Everyone should be able to assert their identity across institutional and national borders, and across time," and that they want to provide "an alternative to individuals lacking safe and reliable access to state-based systems." In other words, vaccines and digital ID are merging together. But how?

Enter quantum dot technology. This new technology is well known, freely discussed in various online tech articles, and is the next step beyond microchipping. As I understand it, visible and invisible ink can be tattooed on someone as they are receiving a vaccine. Embedded in this tattoo is digital technology that verifies they have had said vaccine. Presumably, this could also be technology used to give everyone/anyone a permanent digital ID.

## WO/2020/060606

Now, here is the third-and strangest-number I want to bring to your attention. A short time after Bill Gates stepped down from Microsoft's board of directors, the company filed an international patent for a "cryptocurrency system using body activity data." In layman's terms this means, "a cashless financial system connected to individual people." Some argue that this could just be a patent for technology which allows for smart phones, smart watches, and other wearable technology to connect with a cashless payment system. Of course, that is one logical application. But, when you look at this in view of end-time Bible prophecy, one can't help but connect a few dots. The bottom line is it is a technology that connects individual humans to a database and a cashless system. That is a fact."

I verified all of this information as you can too. These are future events that shall surely come to pass that are not taught in most Christian churches. Things are falling into God's master

plan and I have clearly outlined in in the Christian section of the book below.

## COVID-19 Credentials Initiative (CCI)

Another fascinating article is by Geoffery Grider is the COVID-19 Credentials Initiative:[11] In it he states their goal is to enable a society to return to normal following a worldwide pandemic such as COVID-19 in a controlled, measurable, and privacy-preserving way. For this there needs to be a community passport. He states that a community passport is a digital certificate that lets individuals prove (and request proof from others) that they've recovered after testing negative, have tested positive for antibodies, or have received a vaccination, once one is available. By proving some level of immunity, individuals will be able to begin participating in everyday life again.

---

[11] https:// https://www.covidcreds.com/

# CHAPTER 7

# Viruses

Viruses make constant attempts to invade the perfect host...the human body! Twenty-four hours a day, seven days a week, more than China computer viruses attacking US businesses in a twenty-four-hour period. A super carrier is one person who affects 150 people or more.

The most diverse life form known to man is viruses. There are billions of bacteria in the human body. The number of viruses widely varies. They are harmless until they invade the cell of a human or animal. We've seen house plants get diseases and have to be re-potted or treated with plant medicine or the affected piece has to be broken off. Viruses needs a host and nearly all viruses that can cause a pandemic– comes from animals and insects! One of the main animals to transmit pandemic type viruses to humans is bats. We humans were vegetarians before the Genesis flood. After the flood, God permitted mankind to eat meat:

"1And God blessed Noah and his sons, and said unto them, Be fruitful, and multiply, and replenish the earth. 2And the fear of you and the dread of you shall be upon every beast of the earth, and upon every bird of the heavens; With all wherewith the ground teemeth *(grows), and all the fishes of the sea, into your hand are they delivered. 3Every moving thing that liveth shall be food for you; As the green herb have I given you all. 4But flesh with the life thereof, which is the blood thereof, shall ye not eat," (Genesis 9:1-4, ASV)*

The initial fear and dread God placed on animals that walk, crawl on its belly or fly with wings, were prevented from attacking man that mankind could replenish the earth. God required an animal to be killed with dignity. The animals throat was to be slit, and the heart would pump out the blood until it stopped. God also said that man's life span would be greatly reduced to an average age of 80:

*"10The days of our years are threescore years and ten, Or even by reason of strength fourscore years; Yet is their pride but labor and sorrow; For it is soon gone, and we fly away." (Psalms 90:10)*

So now there are two things at work to naturally shorten mankind's life span: 1) ultraviolet rays from the sun that damage cells and, 2) bad bacteria and viruses.

In the twentieth century alone, more people have died from viruses than all of the wars combined. Every year, the common seasonal flu kills about 646,000 people worldwide.[12] This is a very small percentage considering there are over 7 billion people on the earth. In the US alone, about 12,000 to 61,000 die every year during the flu season.[13] This also is a

---

[12] https://www.medicinenet.com/script/main/art.asp?articlekey=208914.

[13] https://www.cdc.gov/flu/about/burden/index.html.

very small percentage considering the US has over 327 million residents. At the present (9 May 20) we have exceeded our normal seasonal high with Coronavirus deaths (78,200). The numbers are skewed between seasonal flu deaths and actual coronavirus deaths because Medicaid will pay a hospital $13,000 per coronavirus death and $39,000 if the patient goes on a ventilator...good old American greed.

Viruses are fearfully and wonderfully made as is human life, animal life, and plant life. To survive and reproduce, they must invade a cell, not any cell, but they look for the perfect cells. In the case of flu viruses, the perfect cells turn out to be alveoli cells in the lungs. Did you know a billion viruses can fit on the head of an ink pen and viruses are a 100 times smaller than bacteria.[14] Viruses need a host and they actually have no intentions of killing their host, they over reproduce and the results become fatal. Just like viruses, bacteria want to live in its host for the lifetime of the host if it can, and of course, there are billions of good and bad bacteria living in the human body. Also, to ensure its survival, the virus wants to reproduce itself in another host by way of the cough. The human cell is fearfully and wonderfully made! The human cell is an engineering marvel! The human body has in its blood defense mechanisms against bad viruses. Problem is, viruses mutate for their own survival and when that happens we are introduced to new strains.

---

[14] https://www.ncbi.nlm.nih.gov/books/NBK209710/

All of the human sequencing and code for each individual is contained within each human cell. Cells form various tissues and organs for specific functions of the human body, thus the design of Adam and Eve by an all-powerful and knowing God in the Garden of Eden. This truth of life evolving from one man and one woman is confirmed in a report that was produced at Rockefeller University and the University of Basel, Switzerland, published in the Journal of Human Evolution.[15] [16] As a Christian, there is never a need for scientists to back up the divine inspiration of the Holy Bible though it validates what the Holy Scriptures teaches at a time when it was impossible for mankind to know the Genesis account of the creation of Adam and Eve. In addition, seventeen elements of the earth compose the human body–this screams design.[17] Yes, I do hope this information might lead someone to Christ. If not, I won't lose any sleep.

It is not known how long after the flood did mankind begin killing and eating animals. All we do know is that God gave instructions as to how it was to be killed. This information was given to Noah and his three sons and their wives as they began to repopulate the earth. They were vegetarians, and they never killed an animal to eat before the

---

[15] https://www.dailymail.co.uk/news/article-6424407/Every-person-spawned-single-pair-adults-living-200-000-years-ago-scientists-claim.html

[16] https://www.livescience.com/38613-genetic-adam-and-eve-uncovered.html

[17] https://study.com/academy/lesson/comparing-elements-on-earth-to-those-in-the-human-body.html

Genesis flood, just clean animals to offer a sacrifice unto God. We also know that there has been virus pandemics happening after the Genesis flood.

At the creation of Israel as a nation by God, after having led them out of bondage in Egypt and establishing His covenant with them at MT. Sinai, God gave the Israelites a list of clean and unclean animals they were to eat and not eat. Disobedience would result in contracting diseases from animals of which they had no defense. In addition, other nations would see how healthy Israel was and would adopt their diet. Viruses has been killing mankind since he has been eating meat God warned the Israelites to stay away from. In the Wuhan wet market, they were eating bats. Bats are one of the animals God said was unclean to eat. He did not tell Israel *why* beyond they were unclean, it was their *freewill* to obey or disobey.

## Ebola *Manmade* Virus?

The Ebola outbreak was believed to be caused by eating bats and various monkeys.[18] Various monkeys (apes, chimpanzees, etc.) were believed to be the cause of HIV/AIDS... animals forbidden by God to eat. However, more and more studies are pointing to man as the creator of HIV/AIDS by using the kidneys of chimpanzees to make vaccines. Though some animal's autonomy may be similar to

---

[18] https://www.cdc.gov/vhf/ebola/about.html

41

man, God is very clear that all things were made *after its kind*. Sixty percent of viruses comes from animals and seventy-five percent of the sixty percent comes from wild animals. Bats are the main reservoir for Ebola, not monkeys.

## Belgium Congo Trials

Belgium scientists used chimpanzee kidneys to make the Polio vaccine. Between 1957 and 1959, one million Black African's received the secret experimental vaccine. No one was allowed to refuse the vaccine. The WHO criticized the trials. It is believed this is the origins of the AIDS virus. A man-made virus by Belgium scientists and experimented on Black Tribes

in the Republic of Congo. This can be seen in the documentary on Amazon Prime 'The Origins of AIDS.' The evidence is laid out by British Journalist Edward Hooper, in his 1999 book, *The River*. All attempts have been made to keep the truth from coming out about the secret experiment on a population of people no one in political power cared about except God.[19]

As it would take a macro jump (from a horse to a rat) for a chimpanzee to become human...but, if you want to believe you came from a monkey...be my guest; I was created in the image of God.

---

[19] https://www.wired.com/2004/05/film-raises-ire-over-hiv-origins/

Therefore, a virus created in a lab can jump easily from animal to human, but natural evolution would take perhaps hundreds of years. God has given them acids in their mouth and tummy that we don't have. They can eat a rotten corpse and nothing will happen to it, but we would get gravely sick if we cooked and ate spoiled, stinking flesh. We do not see people getting sick from eating a raw steak because the cow is a vegetarian. It is when we eat the meat of wild animals that eat other wild animals that we welcome deadly viruses into our bodies.

Viruses are an invisible enemy and were not made visible until the invention of the microscope in 1590. Satan and devils were not made visible to the world until the Holy Scriptures (Old and New Testament). Viruses are too small to reproduce on their own. They must have a host. Yet, its genetic code is lethal if it can get inside a host.

Like a supercomputer, a supercomputer is a harmless piece of metal and circuit boards with wires until the power button is pressed. Viruses can live on surfaces for a few days just waiting for a host. I have heard upwards of nine days. Viruses actually help reduce the population and reminds mankind of his mortality. Many people around the world will stay away from wet markets as a result of the Coronavirus. Many will stick to eating traditional meats sold in grocery stores and many, all over the world, will continue to go to wet markets for exotic animal foods unless they are shut down.

Now, we must look back and see that H5N1, Asian Avian Flu, started in China, caused by migrating birds (ducks, geese, etc.) infecting domestic birds (chickens, farm raised ducks, geese, etc.) back in 1996, and in humans in 1997. Domestic chickens peck at anything on the ground that might be food and the bird droppings from the wild migrating birds sickened the chickens allowed to free-range and the infected chickens would be put in cages and taken to the wet markets. Birds stacked on top of birds in cages that urinate and drop their poop on the birds below them are the perfect environments to spread viruses.

Pigs eat anything and everything. The H1N1 Swine Flu jumped from infected pigs to humans...also started in China. Then there was SARS (Severe Acute respiratory Syndrome) formally known as SARS coronavirus (SARS-CoV) – virus identified in 2003 (SARS-CoV2 is COVID-19). SARS-CoV is thought to be an animal virus from an as-yet-uncertain animal reservoir, perhaps bats, that spread to other animals (civet cats) and first infected humans in the Guangdong province of southern China in 2002. I hope you get the chance to watch a video of how the wet market operated in Wuhan (wet markets in general).[20] [21] By the way, this is the third SARS out break from China, the last one is mentioned above in 2003 from the lab in Beijing.[22]

---

[20] https://www.youtube.com/watch?v=TPpoJGYlW54

[21] https://www.who.int/ith/diseases/sars/en/

## The Spanish Flu of 1918 and China's Wuhan Coronavirus

Medical scientists cannot predict the exact origins of the Spanish Flu. Its name derived from the soldiers arriving home after WWI. Its origins are in birds. It is 'highly' probably that the Spanish Flu did not originate with soldiers, but from the food source they were provided, mainly poultry. Hundreds of thousands of soldiers returning home from WWI simply became carriers just as the estimated five million people became affected while visiting the epicenter, the Wuhan wet market in China, and got on planes returning home from the epicenter to other locations around the world.

If accurate, given the estimation by the WHO (World Health Organization) that the pandemic began in November of 2019, this would make it a 100-year super bug! It spread from wild birds, various ducks, and geese that migrate in the winter and summer and entered the food chain. Early on, ducks were an unclean animal and not knowing why, Israel simply obeyed the law given to them by God. We can clearly see why these animals were put off limits to the Israelites. The dropping of these migrating birds is eaten by chickens who eat anything on the ground. It was not until 1969 when medical scientists discovered H5N1 (Bird Flu) came from

---

[22] https://www.the-scientist.com/news-analysis/sars-escaped-beijing-lab-twice-50137.

birds. Prior to that, they believed it was a human to human virus.

Droppings from an infected bird, consumed by chickens, infecting it, eaten by humans with the seasonal flu 'probably' was the mode of transmission. We know that it got into the human food system, just how it got in and how it has mutated, leaves us where we are today. Even the bats the Chinese were eating are one of the unclean animals the Israelites were to stay away from. Also, the pig is an unclean animal, yet the Coronavirus has affected Jews and Muslims which do not eat pigs. Rightly so, because virus has no respect a person.

This is a clear indication of human to human transfer of the Coronavirus just as the Flu is spread every year in the winter. The timing is of utmost importance...winter! This virus began in China during 'flu season' thus its symptoms mimicked the common flu until it didn't! The fact that China has poised itself to be a world leader in responding to this pandemic while hording PPE is very suspect. Also, the fact that the head of the WHO, Dr. Tedros Adhanom Ghebreyesus, denied that the virus came from China and China blaming it on U.S. Soldiers, mimics the blame put on French Soldiers though they were just a carrier of the Spanish Flu. It originated where the French Army were getting their food supply...Asian markets.

Make no mistake about it, with world markets collapsing and china holding hostage vital medical information concerning early knowledge and treatment of COVID-19 patients; to include not releasing PPE, and wanting to world to look to 'China' as its savior while attempting to take down America at the same time.

## CHAPTER 8

# Pandemics That Changed History

*The Green New Deal contradicts the Holy Scriptures. God [Jehovah]*
*said Jesus was coming back a 2nd time for 1,000 years (the Millennial*
*Reign of Christ). If the earth can be destroyed in 10 years as the*
*Liberals say, then God is a liar! If God is a liar, then we are not*
*saved by the birth, death, burial, resurrection, and ascension of Jesus*
*back into heaven.*

– Chaplain Zachary

**Pandemics Reduce (help control) the Population**

In the realm of infectious diseases, a pandemic is the worst case scenario. When an epidemic spread beyond a country's borders, that's when the disease officially becomes a pandemic.[23]

As I study the Bible, the Holy Scriptures, people lived for hundreds of years in what was a perfect environment void of

---

[23] https://www.history.com/topics/middle-ages/pandemics-timeline

disease before the great flood in the book of Genesis. This was the best living conditions for the population of the earth as provided by God. There is no mention of disease, just wickedness as a result if sin. Also, mankind was vegetarian and blood from no animal entered his bloodstream. This is a fact that could have only been given to Moses by God.

After the flood, when man began to repopulate the earth, and the eating of meat was allowed by God, did humans began to experience all sorts of diseases. It is the Israelites, by whom an invisible God showed Himself alive to the world, who were given dietary instructions as to what animals were clean and unclean to eat. This would have prevented them from introducing deadly diseases into their system if they obeyed. Their God [Jehovah] also instructed them on how to correctly kill an animal that its blood be drained out because life is in the blood.

I want to list just a few of the worst pandemics in history.

### 430 B.C.: Athens

The earliest recorded pandemic happened during the Peloponnesian War. After the disease passed through Libya, Ethiopia and Egypt, it crossed the Athenian walls as the Spartans laid siege. As much as two-thirds of the population died.

## 541 A.D.: Justinian Plague

First appearing in Egypt, the Justinian plague spread through Palestine and the Byzantine Empire, and then throughout the Mediterranean. Recurrences over the next two centuries eventually killed about 50 million people, 26 percent of the world population. It is believed to be the first significant appearance of the bubonic plague, which features enlarged lymphatic gland and is carried by rats and spread by fleas.

## 1350: The Black Death

Responsible for the death of one-third of the world population, this second large outbreak of the bubonic plague possibly started in Asia and moved west in caravans. Entering through Sicily in 1347 A.D. when plague sufferers arrived in the port of Messina, it spread throughout Europe rapidly killing one-third of the world population.

## 1889: Russian Flu

The first significant flu pandemic started in Siberia and Kazakhstan, traveled to Moscow, and made its way into Finland and then Poland, where it moved into the rest of Europe. By the following year, it had crossed the ocean into North America and Africa. By the end of 1890, 360,000 had died.

## 1918: Spanish Flu

The avian-borne flu that resulted in 50 million deaths worldwide, the 1918 flu was first observed in Europe, the United States and parts of Asia before swiftly spreading around the world. At the time, there were no effective drugs or vaccines to treat this killer flu strain. Wire service reports of a flu outbreak in Madrid in the spring of 1918 led to the pandemic being called the "Spanish flu."

## 1981: HIV/AIDS

First identified in 1981, AIDS destroys a person's immune system, resulting in eventual death by diseases that the body would usually fight off. AIDS was first observed in American gay communities but is believed to have developed from a chimpanzee virus from West Africa in the 1920s. The disease, which spreads through certain body fluids, moved to Haiti in the 1960s, and then New York and San Francisco in the 1970s. Treatments have been developed to slow the progress of the disease, but at least 35 million people worldwide have died of AIDS since its discovery, and in 2020, a cure is yet to be found.

## 2003: SARS

First identified in 2003 after several months of cases, Severe Acute Respiratory Syndrome is believed to have possibly started with bats, spread to cats and then to humans in China, followed by 26 other countries, infecting 8,096 people, with 774 deaths. Quarantine efforts proved effective and by July, the virus was contained and hasn't reappeared since. China was criticized for trying to suppress information about the virus at the beginning of the outbreak.

## 2019: COVID-19

On March 11, 2020, the World Health Organization announced that the COVID-19 virus was officially a pandemic after barreling through 114 countries in three months and infecting over 118,000 people. And the spread wasn't anywhere near finished."

A New Virus No One Is Talking About!

I came across an article that I saw on one of the news channels. It was about a new virus that also has its origins in China. It is a virus associated with pigs by Beth Baumann.[24]

In that article, she stated this new strain of the flu, called G4 EA H1N1, is said to be similar to the swine flu, which came from China in 2009. She goes on to estimate that 10.4 percent of those working in the swine industry are positive for the new strain and that those between the ages of 18 and 35 are most at risk of being infected.

---

[24] http://abq.fm/blog/another-virus-with-the-potential-to-cause-a-pandemic-was-discovered-in-none-other-than-china/

## CHAPTER 9

# Is this a Worldwide Judgement from God?

At what point did not God, the Father, consider Jesus fully human in Mary's womb? – Chaplain Zachary

*"13For thou didst form my inward parts: Thou didst cover me in my mother's womb. 14I will give thanks unto thee; for I am fearfully and wonderfully made: Wonderful are thy works; And that my soul knoweth right well. 15My frame was not hidden from thee, When I was made in secret, And curiously wrought in the lowest parts of the earth. 16Thine eyes did see mine unformed substance; And in thy book they were all written, Even the days that were ordained for me, When as yet there was none of them." (Psalms 139:13-16)*

**Their Fears are Our Fears**

Black Plague: God's punishment?

Because they did not understand the biology of the disease, many people believed that the Black Death was a kind of divine punishment—retribution for sins against God such as greed, blasphemy, heresy, fornication and worldliness.[25]

---

[25] https://www.history.com/topics/middle-ages/black-death.

By this logic, the only way to overcome the plague was to win God's forgiveness. Some people believed that the way to do this was to purge their communities of heretics and other troublemakers—so, for example, many thousands of Jews were massacred in 1348 and 1349. (Thousands more fled to the sparsely populated regions of Eastern Europe, where they could be relatively safe from the rampaging mobs in the cities.)

Some people coped with the terror and uncertainty of the Black Death epidemic by lashing out at their neighbors; others coped by turning inward and fretting about the condition of their own souls.

## Flagellants

Some upper-class men joined processions of flagellants that traveled from town to town and engaged in public displays of penance and punishment: They would beat themselves and one another with heavy leather straps studded with sharp pieces of metal while the townspeople looked on. For 33 1/2 days, the flagellants repeated this ritual three times a day. Then they would move on to the next town and begin the process over again.

Though the flagellant movement did provide some comfort to people who felt powerless in the face of inexplicable tragedy, it soon began to worry the Pope, whose authority the flagellants had begun to usurp. In the face of this papal resistance, the movement disintegrated.

## How Did the Black Death End?

The plague never really ended, *and*…it returned with a vengeance years later. But officials in the Venetian-controlled

port city of Ragusa were able to slow its spread by keeping arriving sailors in isolation until it was clear they were not carrying the disease—creating social distancing that relied on isolation to slow the spread of the disease.

The sailors were initially held on their ships for 30 days (a trentino), a period that was later increased to 40 days, or a quarantine—the origin of the term "quarantine" and a practice still used today.

## Is COVID-19 A Judgment from God?

Never have the world experienced such a pandemic in this age of science and technology where knowledge has been increased. The world has been taken by surprise though we, as students and scholars of the Bible, try to see where we are in the pages of Biblical Prophecy! We are fully understanding this world pandemic as a sign given by Jesus in the book of Matthew as birth pains:

*"3And as he sat on the mount of Olives, the disciples came unto him privately, saying, Tell us, when shall these things be? and what shall be the sign of thy coming, and of the end of the world? 4And*

*Jesus answered and said unto them, Take heed that no man lead you astray. 5For many shall come in my name, saying, I am the Christ; and shall lead many astray. 6And ye shall hear of wars and rumors of wars; see that ye be not troubled: for these things must needs come to pass; but the end is not yet. 7For nation shall rise against nation, and kingdom against kingdom; and there shall be famines and earthquakes in divers (various) places. 8But all these things are the beginning of travail." (Matthew 24:3-8)*

We have had wars (including the currently ongoing *War on Terror*) and rumors of wars (with Russia during the Nuclear Arms Race). Nations has risen up against nations, kingdoms have risen up against kingdoms (WWI & WWII). There have been famines, and pestilences, and earthquakes in various places where earthquakes are rare, so the question is, 'What makes COVID-19 so unique'?

What makes it unique is the worldwide effect it has on nearly every developed nation on the earth–great and small–Christian and non-Christian. There has been four 'God ordained' worldwide judgements recorded in the Old Testament beginning with the Genesis flood, confusion of the people's language at the Tower of Babel, Worldwide Famine (Genesis 41), and the Ten Plagues against the 'gods' of Egypt (Egypt was the first world superpower after the flood).

This section is for those who has spent sufficient time studying the Bible. The human body, at creation, was perfect.

Perfectly designed for the surface of the earth with the deadliest of viruses lying dormant. Make no mistake, bacteria and virus are as fearfully and wonderfully made as the human body, the plant, animal, and insect kingdom...even that pesky mosquito, is fearfully and wonderfully made! God gave the mosquitos wings a piercing sound like no other insect that instantly warns of its presence. As deadly as viruses are and a hundred times smaller than bacteria, they lie dormant until it enters a living cell–that's when all hell breaks loose!

God gave dominion of the earth to Adam, all the works of his hands. God gave mankind the capacity and freewill to choose. If he but obeyed one simple command, not to eat of the knowledge of the tree of good and evil, we'd be chilling in the Garden of Eden right now! Before the worldwide flood, all of mankind and the animal kingdom were vegetarians. Being vegetarians, viruses would not have had the opportunity to enter the human body as easily as meat eaters. Enticed by Satan, Adam exercised his freewill and ate of the forbidden tree–and here we are. Here is where it gets really interesting. Fellowship with God was broken, and the Kingdom of Darkness was introduced into the world. Dominion of the earth defaulted to Satan and mankind was born in sin, under the powers of darkness. The world was Christian in the beginning and will be Christian at the 2nd Coming of Christ"

*"12giving thanks unto the Father, who made us meet to be partakers of the inheritance of the saints in light; 13who delivered us*

out of the power of darkness, and translated us into the kingdom of the Son of his love; 14in whom we have our redemption, the forgiveness of our sins: 15who is the image of the invisible God, the firstborn of all creation; 16for in him were all things created, in the heavens and upon the earth, things visible and things invisible, whether thrones or dominions or principalities or powers; all things have been created through him, and unto him; 17and he is before all things, and in him all things consist. 18And he is the head of the body, the church: who is the beginning, the firstborn from the dead; that in all things he might have the preeminence. 19For it was the good pleasure of the Father that in him should all the fulness dwell; 20and through him

to reconcile all things unto himself, having made peace through the blood of his cross; through him, I say , whether things upon the earth, or things in the heavens. " (Colossians 1:12-20)

And,

"1God, having of old time spoken unto the fathers in the prophets by divers portions and in divers manners, 2hath at the end of these days spoken unto us in his'son, whom he appointed heir of all things, through whom also he made the worlds; 3who being the effulgence of his glory, and the very image of his substance, and upholding all things by the word of his power, when he had made purification of sins, sat down on the right hand of the Majesty on high; 4having become by so much better than the angels, as he hath inherited a more excellent name than they. 5For unto which of the *angels said he at any time, Thou art my Son, This day have I begotten thee? and again, I will be to him a Father, And he shall be to me a Son? 6And when he again bringeth in the firstborn into the world he saith, And let all the angels of God worship him. 7And of the angels he saith, Who maketh his angels winds, And his ministers a flame a fire: 8but of the Son he saith, Thy throne, O God, is for ever and ever; And the sceptre of uprightness is the sceptre of thy kingdom." (Hebrews 1:1-8)*

It is very clear in the New Testament that Jesus is God, the Son of God, and creator of all life on planet earth—including that pesky mosquito! Thus, the world religion was Christianity at creation and shall be Christianity at His 2nd Coming. I can take

you deeper and inform you that though Rome, the One World Ruler at the time of Christ, persecuted Christians, Christianity became the first world religion when Rome, under emperor Constantine, declared Christianity the official religion of Rome. At Jesus' death, Rome was the One World Ruler and One World Government, and Christianity became the One World Religion.

At Jesus' 2nd Coming, there shall indeed be a 'revived' Roman empire unless God is a liar. That's also why the world will not be destroyed in twelve years as the Green New Deal climate warners say. Since God is not a liar, a revived Roman empire shall be in place, maybe the European Union...thus, time picks where Jesus left off. The government in power at His death shall be the government in power at His 2nd Coming. At that time, Jesus shall overthrow the One World Government (revived Roman empire), which is what the Jews wanted Him to do instead of dying on the cross for the sins of the world (Revelation 19). Time stopped–*yet* …kept going. Time shall be–*yet*…is not:

"*31Thou, O king, sawest, and, behold, a great image. This image, which was mighty, and whose brightness was excellent, stood before thee; and the aspect thereof was terrible. 32As for this image, its head was of fine gold, its breast and its arms of silver, its belly and its thighs of brass, 33its legs of iron, its feet part of iron, and part of clay. 34Thou sawest till that a stone was cut out without hands, which smote the image upon its feet that were of iron and clay, and brake them in pieces. 35Then was the iron, the clay, the brass, the silver, and the gold, broken in pieces together, and became like the chaff of the summer threshing-floors; and the wind carried them away, so that no place was found for them: and*

*the stone that smote the image became a great mountain, and filled the whole earth. 36This is the dream; and we will tell the interpretation thereof before the king. 37Thou, O king, art king of kings, unto whom the God of heaven hath given the kingdom, the power, and the strength, and the glory; 38and wheresoever the children of men dwell, the beasts of the field and the birds of the heavens hath he given into thy hand, and hath made thee to rule over them all: thou art the head of gold. 39And after thee shall arise another kingdom inferior to thee; and another third kingdom of brass, which shall bear rule over all the earth. 40And the fourth kingdom shall be strong as iron, forasmuch as iron breaketh in pieces and subdueth all things; and as iron that crusheth all these, shall it break in pieces and crush. 41And whereas thou sawest the feet and toes, part of potters clay, and part of iron, it shall be a divided kingdom; but there shall be in it of the strength of the iron, forasmuch as thou sawest the iron mixed with miry clay. 42And as the toes of the feet were part of iron, and part of clay, so the kingdom shall be partly strong, and partly broken. 43And whereas thou sawest the iron mixed with miry clay, they shall mingle themselves with the seed of men; but they shall not cleave one to another, even as iron doth not mingle with clay. 44And in the days of those kings shall the God of heaven set up a kingdom which shall never be destroyed, nor shall the sovereignty thereof be left to another people; but it shall break in pieces and consume all these kingdoms, and it shall stand for ever. 45Forasmuch as thou sawest that a stone was cut out of the mountain without hands, and that it brake in pieces the iron, the brass, the clay, the silver, and the gold; the great God hath made known to the king what shall come to pass hereafter: and the dream is certain, and the interpretation thereof sure"* (Daniel 2:1-45).

The Powers of Darkness (Satan and the 1/3 fallen angels) at work in the world today, put it in man's mind to create a god (little g) in its image and bow down and worship it *instead* of the Creator. It begs the question, who is greater, the man who gathered the materials and carved the 'god' to be worshipped or the man? Satan was the first angel created with wisdom surpassed only by God who created him (Ezekiel 28:11-19). Satan is able to manipulate thoughts, but he cannot force a person to do anything, that would be demonic possession. However, there is only one person mentioned in the Holy Bible that Satan entered–Judas. He will totally control the antichrist, the leader of the One World Government before the 2nd Coming of Christ (Revelation 13).

Adam and Eve introduced their children to the Creator and worship of the Creator as demonstrated by the sacrifice brought before God by Cain and Abel. There is no mention of Adam and Eve making an offering unto God, maybe God told Cain and Abel to bring an offering, or maybe they brought an offering just to please God? Along the generations, satanic influence caused men to stray from God until the thoughts of men's minds were only evil continually–hello worldwide flood (Genesis 6)!

God started over with Noah and his three sons and their wives once they left the boat. Three men and their wives began to repopulate the earth. This is just a fact: a man and a woman to populate the earth before the flood, and three men and three women to repopulate the earth after the flood (no sterile unions). Worship is once again *only* of the Creator by Noah and his family and once again, as mankind multiply on the face of the earth, satanic influence convinces man to make 'gods' after their image and draw their worship from the Creator to the worship of demonic spirits–fallen angels.

*"7They shall no more offer their sacrifices to demons, after whom they have played the harlot. This shall be a statute forever for them throughout their generations" (Leviticus 17:7, KJV).*

God has not allowed mankind to see angels. So then, how does an invisible demonic spirit (Satan and the 1/3 fallen angels) receive worship...they put it in man's minds to make an image and bow down and worship it, in essence, worshipping devils.

Now, here's where we are in the world today. God will allow mankind to exercise his freewill and follow the unction of demonic spirits and create other gods and worship them. At the same time, they will see that those gods have no power to bless, heal, or save. Everything *good* they blindly attribute it to the god (fallen angel) they worship and everything *bad*, they attribute to their having angered their god some kind of way...thus, the institution of human sacrifice in an attempt to please their god (fallen angels), and at the same time, get rid of unwanted babies.

Hello Abraham! He hears the call of God and of his own freewill, he obeys the voice and leaves the land of Ur. God is going to create a nation to show the real vs the fake. Hello

Israel! Descendants of Abraham, Isaac, and Jacob, whom God changed Jacob's name to Israel; meaning–governed by God. The twelve sons of Jacob are the nation of Israel. God shows His powers against the powerless gods of Egypt through Moses and Aaron (God never intended for Aaron to assist Moses....one plus God is a majority). Not only did God, the Creator of the heavens and the earth and the fullness therein, show the Egyptians...the world Super Power at the time who the real deal was – but He drowned an entire Army in the Red Sea.

Multitudes of people have been seduced by demonic spirits to make images and bow down and worship the image–in essence, worshipping the fallen angels (demonic spirits) whom God the Creator hasn't allowed us to see. So then, how does an invisible angel make himself visible? By putting it in the mind of a man to create an image of itself and bow down and worship it...thus, drawing attention from the true and living God and Creator [Jesus] to itself. Now, this is where we are in the world today, when there are calamities, epidemics, and pandemics in the world, those nations can pray until they are out of breath and never come to the logical conclusion that the deity they worship and sacrifice to...are as powerless as they are.

The purpose of the creation of the nation of Israel, a nation God created thru the obedience of one man, Abraham, and his wife, Sarah, was to bring a Savior into the world. God spilt the

Red Sea for them, led them through the desert wilderness for forty years before splitting the Jordan river and leading them into the land of Canaan. While in the wilderness, He gave them their communal laws and 'dietary' laws. Hello *bat soup*...hello *monkey meat*...hello *Coronavirus*...species God forbid Israel to eat. Many of the species the Chinese eat are forbidden for the Israelites to eat, including monkeys from which HIV/AIDS is believed to have originated. Migrating Geese are also forbidden where we get H1N1–Bird Flu and pigs are forbidden which we get H5N1–Swine Flu.

So now, where are the deities of the world to save their people?

In vain have they been worshipped! I will not make any excuse for Christianity as each religion is wondering where their deity in the midst of is this COVID-19 pandemic. This is the perfect opportunity for the deities of the world to prove to the world that he/she is the real deal! Where is Jesus? Where is Allah? Where is the Buddha? Is this Nirvana? Is this Karma? Where is the Hindu gods? Why are they all silent? Have they no power to save? One thing for sure: religious, non-religious, spiritual, we are all eventually going to die. The question now becomes, 'What consolation is there in death'?

Islam offers no guarantee of salvation unless one becomes a Jihadist. I definitely would not want to bow five times a day in prayer to a god that offered no guarantee of salvation unless I committed Jihad and especially since it teaches that 'Hell' has more women than men. Let me see…if I blow myself up, I will get 72 virgins in Muslim heaven…what about my wife when she dies…must she share them with me…that's 'if' her good outweigh her bad and she makes it to heaven?

*'O women! Give charity, for I have seen that you form the majority of the people of Hell.' They asked, 'Why is that, O Messenger of Allah?' He replied, 'You curse frequently and are ungrateful to your husbands. I have not seen anyone more deficient in intelligence and religious commitment than you. A cautious sensible man could be led astray by some of you.'*[26]

Buddhist teaches they will become a god when they die. If that's the case, why suffer in this world? I would think being a god is way better than being in flesh and blood…just get it over with and become a god. Hindu teaches I will be reincarnated when I die, back on this earth, as some other lifeform–I could return to life as a *roach* if I was a bad person! What non-sense, where is the comfort in death as a Hindu?

Communist leaders are a god unto themselves. But wait a minute, the Christian God, Jesus, came from heaven and died on the cross for my sins so that if I die from cancer, car wreck, heart attack, COVID-19…I have a one-way ticket to heaven. A

---

[26] https://islamqa.info/en/answers/21457/more-women-in-hell-than-men

place where people who have had 'near death' experiences had a glimpse of heaven and have described it as a very real place and the abode of God. For those of you that can understand that very real scenario–sweet! With the permission to eat meat after the flood, mankind has been putting viruses in his system to this day.

If the Judeo-Christian God of whose son I am needs to be defended, then He is not God. Many Christian bible scholars would label this as a 'birth pain' because of its global effect. This is considered a 'type' of worldwide judgment coming upon the earth. Well, you say, I don't believe in that *hocus-pocus*...and that's ok because the Holy Bible is written to believers in Jesus Christ who has exercised a 'mustard seed' of faith to enter the Kingdom of Heaven:

*"13Which things also we speak, not in words which man's wisdom teacheth, but which the Spirit teacheth; combining spiritual things with spiritual words. 14Now the natural man receiveth not the things of the Spirit of God: for they are foolishness unto him; and he cannot know them, because they are spiritually judged. 15But he that is spiritual judgeth all things, and he himself is judged of no man. 16For who hath known the mind of the Lord, that he should instruct him? But we have the mind of Christ." (1 Corinthians 2:13-16)*

The Holy Bible is 'given' to the world that the world might believe and be saved. With that said, the Coronavirus is a 'type' of worldwide judgment to come upon all of the earth as did the flood recorded in the book of Genesis.

The Coronavirus 'shock' happened as did the worldwide flood in that, the world was going about its business when disaster came and caught the inhabitants by surprise. Jesus speaks of His 'Second Coming/Advent' in the same way the worldwide flood and the Coronavirus took the world by surprise:

*"38For as in those days which were before the flood they were eating and drinking, marrying and giving in marriage, until the day that Noah entered into the ark, 39and they knew not until the flood came, and took them all away; so shall be the coming of the Son of man." (Matthew 24:38-39)*

The world is in a state of shock as the world struggles to get a handle on the spread of the Coronavirus. In this same manner

shall the judgments of the book of Revelation come upon the world and then shall come the end of 'human history' where men and women are elected Presidents, Kings/Queens, Prime Ministers, Supreme Leaders, Dictators, etc., etc. this is the clear meaning of 'the end of the age' as spoken of by the Prophets, the Apostles, and Jesus:

*"14And this gospel of the kingdom shall be preached in the whole world for a testimony unto all the nations; and then shall the end come." (Matthew 24:14)*

This 'type' of worldwide judgment is laid upon Christian and non-Christian which is why I ponder the meaning. I am reminded of the 'Ten Plagues' against Egypt in which the first three plagues effected both Hebrew (Jews) and Gentile (non-Jews). The first of which was the turning of water into blood. This was matched by the magicians of Egypt and had no effect on the Pharaoh whatsoever.

The second was the plague of 'frogs' which, as you can imagine, would be a very grievous plague mostly because of the sounds hundreds of thousands, if not millions, of frogs from the Nile river would be making 24/7. This sign was duplicated by the Egyptian magicians simply to prove to Moses and Aaron that there was nothing special about the God of the Hebrews.

The third plague was the plague of 'lice.' This plague involved direct contact between insect and human, making both Hebrew and Egyptian very uncomfortable. This plague would, as with the first two, would have stopped all social events, but the people would have still been required to go to work, unlike the Coronavirus that has caused many to stay home and practice 'social distancing' to help stop the spread.

Where things get very interesting is here, the fourth through tenth plague, where I and other bible prophecy students...*btw*...I hope you become a student of bible prophecy after reading this book and begin searching the Holy scriptures for answers. It really is incredible to wonder how this worldwide pandemic fits into God's plan. Be not confused, the Holy Bible 'is' the oracle of God. Despite all of the doubters, fulfilment of 'Bible Prophecy' is the infallible proof of the Holy Scriptures...Old Testament and New Testament. Remember, this book of instructions is only for those who have the *Holy Spirit*. He is only given to those who have accepted Jesus as our Lord and Savior. All others truly are not fazed by the contents of the Holy Bible, thus their reliance on science, technology, and the government.

Let me say upfront, politicians are writing laws that take away the guilt of abortion and LGBTQ+ lifestyles. These are the two major moral issues facing the world, which **'words'** remove guilt and fear of God. I must include the word 'liberal' politicians because the Holy Bible is **'conservative.'** There is absolutely nothing liberal about the Holy Scriptures given to *holy men* as they were moved by the *Holy Spirit*.

*"15but like as he who called you is holy, be ye yourselves also holy in all manner of living; 16because it is written, Ye shall be holy; for I am holy." (1 Peter 1:15)*

This verse eliminates any 'liberalism' in Christianity. Thus, followers of Christianity should **'only'** be conservative. More importantly, the infallibility of the Holy Scriptures has its divine stamp of approval in 2 Peter 1:16-21:

*"16For we did not follow cunningly devised fables, when we made known unto you the power and coming of our Lord Jesus Christ, but we were eyewitnesses of his majesty. 17For he received from God the Father honor and glory, when there was borne such a voice to him by the Majestic Glory, This is my beloved Son, in whom I am well pleased: 18and this voice we ourselves heard borne out of heaven, when we were with him in the holy mount. 19And we have the word of prophecy made more sure; whereunto ye do well that ye take heed, as unto a lamp shining in a dark place, until the day dawn, and the day-star arise in your hearts: 20knowing this first, that no prophecy of scripture is of private interpretation. 21For no prophecy ever came by the will of man: but men spake from God, being moved by the Holy Spirit." (2 Peter 1;16-21)*

All of the New Testament writers were *eyewitnesses!* As Christians, we do not need any proof from scientists about the content of the Holy Scriptures because only God can tell the future in advance. Now, concerning the fourth thru tenth plagues of Egypt, God was not only showing the Egyptians that their gods (little...g) had no power to save, but that the God of the Hebrews were indeed the true and living God of all creation–so much so, that many of the Egyptians believed and left Egypt with the children of the covenant God made with Abraham. The tenth plague could have killed the first born of the descendants of Jacob had they not believed and put blood upon their door posts as instructed by Moses. Since they did, the death angel only killed all of the first born of Egypt.

What's most fascinating is how God is able to keep those that are His from the coming calamity that shall surely come upon the world. He proved it in the fourth thru tenth plagues that only the Egyptians experienced...the plagues of 'Flies, Livestock, Boils, Hail, Locusts, Darkness, and the First Born.' Depending on your relationship with God, one can easily see how God could protect His people while others suffered, but this was all new to the Israelites, they were experiencing God's miraculous powers for the first time.

All of the ten plagues were against the 'gods' of Egypt whom they faithfully worshipped and served only to discover that they had no power. Since the Coronavirus is attacking both Christian and non-Christian, this virus would coincide with the first three plagues of Egypt. The only difference is the New Testament classification of a virus of this magnitude as 'birth pains.' Also, as of 9 Nov 20, this virus is looking more and more like a lab experiment gone wrong.

Following pestilence in the book of Matthew, Chapter 24, is mentioned notable earthquake in places that do not normally experience earthquakes. Whether one that will rattle the world as the Coronavirus has done will happen, I don't know. We do know that there shall be earthquakes as part of the birth pangs! The worst recorded earthquake in the world was in 1960, in Chile, known as the 'Valdivia' earthquake (Spanish: Terremoto de Valdivia) or the Great Chilean earthquake (Gran Terremoto de Chile) on 22 May 1960. It was the most powerful earthquake ever recorded. Various studies have placed it at 9.4–9.6 on the magnitude scale.[27]

---

[27] https://en.wikipedia.org/wiki/1960_Valdivia_earthquake.

## CHAPTER 10

# Birth Pains Intensifying

*In 2020, Liberal Democrats would demand Barabbas be released instead of Jesus*

– Chaplain Zachary

*"4Now the word of Jehovah came unto me, saying, 5Before I formed thee in the belly I knew thee, and before thou camest forth out of the womb I sanctified thee; I have appointed thee a prophet unto the nations." (Jeremiah 1:4-5)*

## The Worldwide Seal Judgements

Leave no doubt in your mind, this COVID-19 Pandemic is a precursor to the worldwide judgment that is to come. Before the Genesis flood, God judged the whole world at the same time. After the flood, God judged nations individually. The first we read of God judging nations every 400 years is with Abraham, when God tells him that He cannot give him the land of Canaan because the iniquity (sin) of the Amorites is not yet full:

"*6And he believed in Jehovah; and he reckoned it to him for righteousness. 7And he said unto him, I am Jehovah that brought thee out of Ur of the Chaldees, to give thee this land to inherit it. 8And he said, O Lord Jehovah, whereby shall I know that I shall inherit it? 9And he said unto him, Take me a heifer three years old, and a she-goat three years old, and a ram three years old, and a turtle-dove, and a young pigeon. 10And he took him all these, and divided them in the midst, and laid each half over against the other: but the birds divided he not. 11And the birds of prey came down upon the carcasses, and Abram drove them away. 12And when the sun was going down, a deep sleep fell upon Abram; and, lo, a horror of great darkness fell upon him. 13And he said unto Abram, Know of a surety that thy seed shall be sojourners in a land that is not theirs, and shall serve them; and they shall afflict them four hundred years; 14and also that nation, whom they shall serve, will I judge: and afterward shall they come out with great substance. 15But thou shalt go to thy fathers in peace; thou shalt be buried in a good old age. 16And in the fourth generation they shall come hither again; for the iniquity of the Amorite is not yet full.*" (Genesis 15:6-16)

Not only that, after the 400 years, Egypt was judged. Egypt turned on Israel who saved them from extinction during the worldwide famine. This is proof from early on that each generation gets more wicked than before. I have no doubt that Satan put it in the spirit of latter Pharaohs to enslave Israel. God spoke of this 400 years before it happened, then God judged Egypt by 1) proving to the Egyptians that their gods had no power to save *nor* battle against Jehovah, 2) He keeps His covenant promises, and 3) Prophecy. God spoke in advance that which would surely come to pass exactly as He said it.

This Pandemic is a warning to the world–mostly to true Christians, who believe there is **absolutely** no other way to heaven but trough Jesus the Christ, Son of God, Son of David, Son of the Virgin Mary. The first world judgment that will come upon a global leader of a one world government (which this pandemic gives a glimpse of) shall be a great earthquake like never before:

*"12And I saw when he opened the sixth seal, and there was a great earthquake; and the sun became black as sackcloth of hair, and the whole moon became as blood; 13and the stars of the heaven fell unto the earth, as a fig tree casteth her unripe figs when she is shaken of a great wind. 14And the heaven was removed as a scroll when it is rolled up; and every mountain and island were moved out of their places." (Revelation 6:12-14)*

This is just a 'get ready' for what's next! Check this out:

*"15And the kings of the earth, and the princes, and the chief captains, and the rich, and the strong, and every bondman and freeman, hid themselves in the caves and in the rocks of the mountains; 16and they say to the mountains and to the rocks, Fall on us, and hide us from the face of him that sitteth on the throne, and*

*from the wrath of the Lamb: 17for the great day of their wrath is come; and who is able to stand?" (Revelation 6:15-17)*

I know, I know…this is a bunch of *hocus-pocus* to non-Christians. Notice that the people on the earth acknowledge God in their calamity. God is completely removed from government and regulated only to the church and people's private homes, yet God is not fazed by it. Heaven is only going to be filled with those who want to be there. These are all Christ rejecting people because the 'Body of Christ' has been removed in the Rapture. The Holy Bible is very clear, once the Church, the 'Bride of Christ' is taken out of this world to heaven, it shall be followed

by a period of seven years where God grants the world what it desires…removal of His influence. Satan will be in total control until the end of the seven-year period of time known as the Tribulation Period. The last 3 1/2 years are clearly interpreted as the Great Tribulation or Time of Jacob's troubles or Abomination of Desolation.

The second world judgment to come on mankind will be a combined thunderstorm and earthquake:

*"1And when he opened the seventh seal, there followed a silence in heaven about the space of half an hour. 2And I saw the seven angels that stand before God; and there were given unto them seven trumpets. 3And another angel came and stood over the altar, having a golden censer; and there was given unto him much incense, that he*

*should add it unto the prayers of all the saints upon the golden altar which was before the throne. 4And the smoke of the incense, with the prayers of the saints, went up before God out of the angel's hand. 5And the angel taketh the censer; and he filled it with the fire of the altar, and cast it upon the earth: and there followed thunders, and voices, and lightnings, and an earthquake." (Revelation 8:1-5)*

I perceive flooding from the thunderstorm will greatly prevent the saving of many lives. There will be absolutely no stopping these judgments once they begin. Mankind has rejected his creator and worshipped the creature (themselves) more than the creator:

*"18For the wrath of God is revealed from heaven against all ungodliness and unrighteousness of men, who hinder the truth in unrighteousness; 19because that which is known of God is manifest in them; for God manifested it unto hem. 20For the invisible things of him since the creation of the world are clearly seen, being perceived through the things that are made, even his everlasting power and divinity; that they may be without excuse: 21because that, knowing God, they glorified him not as God, neither gave thanks; but became vain in their reasonings, and their senseless heart was darkened. 22Professing themselves to be wise, they became fools, 23and changed the glory of the incorruptible God for the likeness of an image of corruptible man, and of birds, and four-footed beasts, and creeping things. 24Wherefore God gave them up in the lusts of their hearts unto uncleanness, that their bodies should be dishonored among themselves: 25for that they exchanged the truth of*

*God for a lie, and worshipped and served the creature rather than the Creator, who is blessed for ever. Amen. 26For this cause God gave them up unto vile passions: for their women changed the natural use into that which is against nature: 27and likewise also the men, leaving the natural use of the woman, burned in their lust one toward another, men with men working unseemliness, and receiving in themselves that recompense of their error which was due. 28And even as they refused to have God in their knowledge, God gave them up unto a reprobate mind, to do those things which are not fitting; 29being filled with all unrighteousness, wickedness, covetousness, maliciousness; full of envy, murder, strife, deceit, malignity; whisperers, 30backbiters, hateful to God, insolent, haughty, boastful, inventors of evil things, disobedient to parents, 31without understanding, covenant-breakers, without natural affection, unmerciful: 32who, knowing the ordinance of God, that they that practice such things are worthy of death, not only do the same, but also consent with them that practice them." (Romans 1:18-32).*

We can clearly see how **'words'** remove guilt, but mankind is still very guilty before God. In God's wrath, the Christ rejection people prayed for the mountains to hide them from the wrath of He who sits on the Throne, the wrath of the Lamb (Jesus). Leave no doubt in your mind, Jesus is doing all of the judging:

*"21For as the Father raiseth the dead and giveth them life, even so the Son also giveth life to whom he will. 22For neither doth the*

*Father judge any man, but he hath given all judgment unto the Son; 23that all may honor the Son, even as they honor the Father. He that honoreth not the Son honoreth not the Father that sent him."* (John 5:21-23)

Many people believe that they will go to heaven when they die because they see themselves as a good person. Never mind what God says, that 'all' have sinned and can only be saved by accepting Jesus as their Lord and Savior.

## CHAPTER 11

# The Coming One World Government

*God [Jehovah] is Holy. He is NOT Liberal. NO part of the Holy Scriptures in the Holy Bible supports Liberalism. The Holy Bible is Conservative. There should only be conservative Christians.*

– Chaplain Zachary

It is coming and there is nothing we can do about it. God cannot lie. I see it so clearly now with the *far-left* liberal Democratic Party. With the Marxist organizations like BLM and Antifa and Democratic Mayors and Governors not arresting rioters and looters, but allowing them to destroy property, take over whole city blocks-the stage is set! All that is needed is a liberal far left Democrat President and a majority Senate Democrat to end the Filibuster that the minority Republicans cannot stop their Green New Deal and other anti-Christ agenda.

What we are witnessing is worship of the creature in Joe Biden's candidacy for President more than worship of the

Creator. the Democratic Party, in 2020, would ask for Barabbas instead of Jesus! What we can do with much prayer is support President Trump's bid for reelection. This will prolong Satan's agenda for world domination for four more years. President's Trump hands will be tied if he does not have a majority of Republicans in both the Senate and Congress. It is a mighty spiritual warfare we are in, and can win, at least for the next four years.

God has told us of the world rulers in the book of Daniel which happened just as the Holy Scriptures said, beginning with Babylon as the first world ruler, followed by Medo-Persia,

Greece, and Rome. At the birth of Jesus, Rome ruled the world. At the death of Jesus, Christianity would become the world religion of Rome. Since Rome was the World Ruler, then Christianity became the World Religion. Satan's plan of stomping out Christianity was once again thwarted by God.

"1In the first year of Belshazzar king of Babylon Daniel had a dream and visions of his head upon his bed: then he wrote the dream and told the sum of the matters. 2Daniel spake and said, I saw in my vision by night, and, behold, the four winds of heaven brake forth upon the great sea. 3And four great beasts came up from the sea, diverse one from another. 4The first was like a lion, and had eagle's wings: I beheld till the wings thereof were plucked, and it was lifted up from the earth, and made to stand upon two feet as a man; and a *man's heart was given to it. 5And, behold, another beast, a second, like to a bear; and it was raised up on one side, and three ribs were in its mouth between its teeth: and they said thus unto it, Arise, devour much flesh. 6After this I beheld, and, lo, another, like a leopard, which had upon its back four wings of a bird; the beast had also four heads; and dominion was given to it. 7After this I saw in the night-visions, and, behold, a fourth beast, terrible and powerful, and strong exceedingly; and it had great iron teeth; it devoured and brake in pieces, and stamped the residue with its feet: and it was diverse from all the beasts that were before it; and it had ten horns. 8I considered the horns, and, behold, there came up among them another horn, a little one, before which three of the first horns were plucked up by the roots: and, behold, in this horn were eyes like the eyes of a man, and a mouth speaking great things (arrogance)." (Daniel 7:1-8)*

God gave the detail in pinpoint accuracy. The succession of 'world' rulers that only further proved the Bible is the *oracle* of God! The bible speaks of a final world ruler and one world government before the second coming of Christ. A Joe Biden presidency will not stand up to China nor Russia nor Iran and will be a puppet in their hands and the hands of the United Nations. America and nine other nations will submit to a One World Leader and a One World Government.

### Daniel's Vision Interpreted

*"15As for me, Daniel, my spirit was grieved in the midst of my body, and the visions of my head troubled me. 16I came near unto*

*one of them that stood by, and asked him the truth concerning all this. So he told me, and made me know the interpretation of the things. 17These great beasts, which are four, are four kings, that shall arise out of the earth. 18But the saints of the Most High shall receive the kingdom, and possess the kingdom for ever, even for ever and ever. 19Then I desired to know the truth concerning the fourth beast, which was diverse from all of them, exceeding terrible, whose teeth were of iron, and its nails of brass; which devoured, brake in pieces, and stamped the residue with its feet; 20and concerning the ten horns that were on its head, and the other horn which came up, and before which three fell, even that horn that had eyes, and a mouth that spake great things, whose look was more stout than its fellows. 21I beheld, and the same horn made war with the saints, and prevailed against them; 22until the ancient of days came, and judgment was given to the saints of the Most High, and the time came that the saints possessed the kingdom. 23Thus he said, The fourth beast shall be a fourth kingdom upon earth, which shall be diverse from all the kingdoms, and shall devour the whole earth, and shall tread it down, and break it in pieces. 24And as for the ten horns, out of this kingdom shall ten kings arise: and another shall arise after them; and he shall be diverse from the former, and he shall put down three kings. 25And he shall speak words against the Most High, and shall wear out the saints of the Most High; and he shall think to change the times and the law; and they shall be given into his hand until a time and times and half a time. 26But the judgment shall be set, and they shall take away his dominion, to consume and to destroy it unto the end. 27And the kingdom and the dominion, and the greatness of the kingdoms under the whole heaven, shall be given to the people of the saints of the Most High: his kingdom is an everlasting kingdom, and all dominions shall serve and obey him. 28Here is the end of the matter. As for me, Daniel, my thoughts much troubled me, and my countenance was changed in me: but I kept the matter in my heart." (Daniel 7:15-28)*

In verse 23, it is clearly speaking of Rome, the last World Ruler. Rome put down any aggression swiftly and ruled with an iron hand. Verse 24 speaks of the last World Ruler before the 2nd Coming of Christ. The world will be divided into ten nations of which the Anti-Christ will defeat three of those nations to such a degree that none of the other seven nations dare challenge his authority. He actually sounds like China's bully, Xi Jinping, who attacks any nation that tries to defy China dominating the world.

## The Last 'One World Ruler' Shall Exalt Himself

*"36And the king shall do according to his will; and he shall exalt himself, and magnify himself above every god, and shall speak marvellous things against the God of gods; and he shall prosper till the indignation be accomplished; for that which is determined shall be done. 37Neither shall he regard the gods of his fathers, nor the desire of women, nor regard any god; for he shall magnify himself above all. 38But in his place shall he honor the god of fortresses; and a god whom his fathers knew not shall he honor with gold, and*

*silver, and with precious stones, and pleasant things. 39And he shall deal with the strongest fortresses by the help of a foreign god: whosoever acknowledgeth him he will increase with glory; and he shall cause them to rule over many, and shall divide the land for a price. 40And at the time of the end shall the king of the south contend with him; and the king of the north shall come against him like a whirlwind, with chariots, and with horsemen, and with many ships; and he shall enter into the countries, and shall overflow and pass through. 41He shall enter also into the glorious land, and many countries' shall be overthrown; but these shall be delivered out of his hand: Edom, and Moab, and the chief of the children of Ammon. 42He shall stretch forth his hand also upon the countries; and the land of Egypt shall not escape. 43But he shall have power over the treasures of gold and of silver, and over all the precious things of Egypt; and the Libyans and the Ethiopians shall be at his steps. 44But tidings out of the east and out of the north shall trouble him; and he shall go forth with great fury to destroy and utterly to sweep away many. 45And he shall plant the tents of his palace between the sea and the glorious holy mountain; yet he shall come to his end, and none shall help him." (Daniel 11:36-45)*

In verse 37, it is clear the last world ruler 'anti-Christ' will not desire women. This is an indication that he might be Gay. The only other explanation is that he is imitating Jesus who did not have sexual contact with a woman when He walked the earth during His 33 years. He will be an atheist; the perfect man Satan will groom for the position and Satan will give him his powers.

"*1and he stood upon the sand of the sea. And I saw a beast coming up out of the sea, having ten horns, and seven heads, and on his horns ten diadems, and upon his heads names of blasphemy. 2And the beast which I saw was like unto a leopard, and his feet were as the feet of a bear, and his mouth as the mouth of a lion: and the dragon gave him his power, and his throne, and great authority. 3And I saw one of his heads as though it had been smitten unto death; and his death-stroke was healed: and the whole earth wondered after the beast; 4and they worshipped the dragon, because he gave his authority unto the beast; and they worshipped the beast, saying, Who is like unto the beast? And who is able to war with him? 5and there was given to him a mouth speaking great things and blasphemies; and there was given to him authority to continue forty and two months. 6And he opened his mouth for blasphemies against God, to blaspheme his name, and his tabernacle (dwelling place), even them that dwell in the heaven. 7And it was given unto him to make war with the saints,*

*and to overcome them: and there was given to him authority over every tribe and people and tongue and nation. 8And all that dwell on the earth shall worship him, every one whose name hath not been written from the foundation of the world in the book of life of the Lamb that hath been slain. 9If any man hath an ear, let him hear. 10If any man is for captivity, into captivity he goeth: if any man shall kill with the sword, with the sword must he be killed. Here is the patience and the faith of the saints." (Revelation 13:1-10).*

In verse 4, we can clearly see that the last world ruler will be an atheist and not desire women and have the power of Satan to solidify his rule (just not sure if he is Gay). He will be anti-Semitic and anti-Christian as Islam is today. The scriptures are very clear that he will attack Israel and only a remnant shall be saved as well as Christians who do not take the *mark* of the Beast (Anti-Christ/World Ruler) nor his *number* nor his *name*. It is so exciting to see these things falling into place right before our eyes!

The tenure of the final world ruler shall be for seven years, then he shall be defeated by Jesus at His 2nd Coming.

*"13I saw in the night-visions, and, behold, there came with the clouds of heaven one like unto a son of man, and he came even to the ancient of days, and they brought him near before him. 14And there was given him dominion, and glory, and a kingdom, that all the peoples, nations, and languages should serve him: his dominion is an everlasting dominion, which shall not pass away, and his kingdom that which shall not be destroyed." (Daniel 7:13-14)*

Verse 14 makes clear reference to the 2nd Coming of Jesus to the earth as King Jesus. Notice in verse 14, that Jesus' kingdom here on the earth shall never be destroyed. The earth will become the new heaven where Jesus and the Father will dwell when He creates a new Jerusalem, a new heaven, and a new earth.

"*1And I saw a new heaven and a new earth: for the first heaven and the first earth are passed away; and the sea is no more. 2And I saw the holy city, new Jerusalem, coming down out of heaven of God, made ready as a bride adorned for her husband. 3And I heard a great voice out of the throne saying, Behold, the tabernacle of God is with men, and he shall dwell with them, and they shall be his peoples, and God himself shall be with them, and be their God: 4and he shall wipe away every tear from their eyes; and death shall be no more; neither shall there be mourning, nor crying, nor pain, any more: the first things are passed away.*

*5And he that sitteth on the throne said, Behold, I make all things new. And he saith, Write: for these words are faithful and true. 6And he said unto me, They are come to pass. I am the Alpha and the Omega, the beginning and the end. I will give unto him that is athirst of the fountain of the water of life freely. 7He that overcometh shall inherit these things; and I will be his God, and he shall be my son. 8But for the fearful, and unbelieving, and abominable, and murderers, and fornicators, and sorcerers, and idolaters, and all liars, their part'shall be in the lake that burneth with fire and brimstone; which is the second death.*" (*Revelation 21:1-8*)

Verse 3 is very clear that God will once again dwell with mankind as He did in the Garden of Eden and at Jesus' 1st

Coming as the Son of the Virgin Mary. Verse 8 is also very clear that LGBTQ+ will not be saved as God calls that lifestyle an abomination. This also includes those who life a lifestyle of fornication and adultery without repentance.

The point of all that I have presented is for us to see how all of these things God has said is lining up with the Holy Scriptures. As Christians, we *unshakably* have the very Oracle (word) of God and the Democrats will usher America into the system of the One World Ruler, One World Government, God has already told us is going to come to pass.

## CHAPTER 12

# Commercial Babylon's (Stock Market) Destruction

*Islam – NO guarantee of salvation unless you become a Jihadist. It is just a Master/Slave relationship. Muslims cannot call Allah – Father. Allah has not sons…very true!*

*God the Father [Jehovah] has a Son named Jesus and*

*'All' who call on the name of Jesus shall be saved!*

*– Chaplain Zachary (Romans 10:8-13)*

I want to interject that God *will* attack the economic structure of governments! As America had the greatest economy in the world before January 2020, before the spread of the Coronavirus and the closing of business…God will destroy the economic structure of Governments as the Coronavirus did. The world will go from a hot economy to bankrupt–overnight! This is clearly taught in the book of Revelation:

*"1After these things I saw another angel coming down out of heaven, having great authority; and the earth was lightened with his*

*glory. 2And he cried with a mighty voice, saying, Fallen, fallen is Babylon the great, and is become a habitation of demons, and a hold of every unclean spirit, and a hold of every unclean and hateful bird. 3For by the wine of the wrath of her fornication all the nations are fallen; and the kings of the earth committed fornication with her, and the merchants of the earth waxed rich by the power of her wantonness. 4And I heard another voice from heaven, saying, Come forth, my people, out of her, that ye have no fellowship with her sins, and that ye receive not of her plagues: 5for her sins have reached even unto heaven, and God hath remembered her iniquities. 6Render unto her even as she rendered, and double unto her the double according to her works: in the cup which she mingled, mingle unto her double. 7How much soever she glorified herself, and waxed wanton, so much give her of torment and mourning: for she saith in her heart, I sit a queen, and am no widow, and shall in no wise see mourning. 8Therefore in one day shall her plagues come, death, and mourning, and famine; and she shall be utterly burned with fire; for strong is the Lord God who judged her. 9And the kings of the earth, who committed fornication and lived wantonly with her, shall weep and wail over her, when they look upon the smoke of her burning, 10standing afar off for the fear of her torment, saying, Woe, woe, the great city, Babylon, the strong city! for in one hour is thy judgment come. 11And the merchants of the earth weep and mourn over her, for no man buyeth their merchandise any more; 12merchandise of gold, and silver, and precious stone, and pearls, and fine linen, and purple, and silk, and scarlet; and all thyine wood, and every vessel of ivory, and every vessel made of most precious wood, and of brass, and iron, and marble; 13and cinnamon, and spice, and incense, and ointment, and frankincense, and wine, and oil, and fine flour, and wheat, and cattle, and sheep; and merchandise of horses and chariots and slaves; and souls of men. 14And the fruits which thy soul lusted after are gone from thee, and all things that were dainty and sumptuous are perished from thee, and men'shall find them no more at all. 15The merchants of these things, who were made rich by her, shall stand afar off for the fear of her torment, weeping and mourning; 16saying, Woe, woe, the great city, she that was arrayed in fine linen and purple and scarlet, and decked with gold and precious stone and pearl! 17for in an hour so great riches is made desolate. And every shipmaster, and every one that saileth any wither, and mariners, and as many as gain their living by sea, stood afar off, 18and cried out as they looked upon the smoke of her burning, saying, What city is like the great city? 19And they cast dust on their heads, and cried, weeping and mourning, saying, Woe, woe, the great city, wherein all that had their ships in the sea were made rich by reason of her costliness! for in one hour is she made desolate." (Revelation 18:1-19)*

We can clearly see how the COVID-19 virus is a perfect 'type' of worldwide judgment on the world *economic* structure. As the Great American Depression of 1929 bankrupted America – the world will experience the same devastation–all in one day! Eleven thousand banks fell in America during the 1929 Great Depression. All of the banks will be invested in the hottest economy at the time of the judgments. Their banks will fail, causing all, *great* and *small,* to lose everything!

God sees what we do not see and things we do not even hear of. Things done in secret that He shall judge at the economic collapse of the world. There are secret societies of the very rich and politically powerful that operate in the background…just like Satan and his kingdom of darkness. One such group is the Secret Society of Bohemian Grove in Southern California.[28]

There you will see well-known men *before* they became President of the United States. The political leaders of tomorrow had to be approved beforehand. This was to ensure that the country moved in a certain direction. That direction clearly is towards a 'One World Government' God warns of in the prophetic books of Daniel and the book of Revelation. During the 2016, Presidential Elections, the 'Deep States' showed themselves. President Trump, it seems, was not to be elected…by any means necessary! And if elected, he must be impeached and not allowed to serve a second term. These secret societies are clearly visible to God and though we feel that we don't have a voice (except on conservative news outlets) – we have a vote!

---

[28] https://www.washingtonpost.com/blogs/blogpost/post/bohemian-grove-where-the-rich-and-powerful-go-to-misbehave/2011/06/15/AGPV1sVH_blog.html

Because of the collapse of the world economic system, food sources must be controlled, thus the 'One World Leader' shall impose a 'mark' that no one can buy or sell without. God warns of those who take that 'mark' that they have sealed their future in–Hell!

"*11And I saw another beast coming up out of the earth; and he had two horns like unto lamb, and he spake as a dragon. 12And he exerciseth all the authority of the first beast in his sight. And he maketh the earth and them dwell therein to worship the first beast, whose death-stroke was healed. 13And he doeth great signs, that he should even make fire to come down out of heaven upon the earth in the sight of men. 14And he deceiveth them that dwell on the earth by reason of the signs which it was given him to do in the sight of the beast; saying to them that dwell on the earth, that they should make an image to the beast who hath the stroke of the sword and lived. 15And it was given unto him to give breath to it, even to the image to the breast, that the image of the beast should both speak, and cause that as many as should not worship the image of the beast should be killed. 16And he causeth all, the small and the great, and the rich and the poor, and the free and the bond, that there be given them a mark on their right hand, or upon their forehead; 17and that no man should be able to buy or to sell, save he that hath the mark, even the name of the beast or the number of his name. 18Here is wisdom. He that hath understanding, let him count the number of the beast; for it is the number of a man: and his number is Six hundred and sixty and six." (Rev 13:11-18)*

Taking the 'Mark' shows allegiance to Satan. Being willing to die for Christ means not taking the *mark*, which means new believers must flee to the wilderness, or try to hideout and steal food for 3 ½ years. We have just read how those who refuse to take the mark will be killed. The book of Revelation adds more details of their deaths:

*"4And I saw thrones, and they sat upon them, and judgment was given unto them: and I saw the souls of them that had been beheaded for the testimony of Jesus, and for the word of God, and such as worshipped not the beast, neither his image, and received not the mark upon their forehead and upon their hand; and they lived, and reigned with Christ a thousand years. 5The rest of the dead lived not until the thousand years should be finished. This is the first resurrection. 6Blessed and holy is he that hath part in the first resurrection: over these the second death hath no power; but they shall be priests of God and of Christ, and shall reign with him a thousand years." (Revelation 20:4-6)*

God has told us before it happens, that those who come to faith in Christ after the Church is taken out in the Rapture, will be beheaded if they do not take the 'Mark of the Beast, nor his Number, nor his Name.' There is one religious group that beheads people – Islam. Islam will play an important role in killing Jews and Christians who do not take the *mark*. Islam already is 'Anti-Christ'...they deny Jesus is the Son of God. Doesn't matter, all Christ rejecting people will open up their eyes in *Hell!* So then, these secret societies shall be judged when God judges what He calls *Commercial Babylon*. Commercial Babylon could be New York. When the World Trade Center was rebuilt, a name was solicited for it. The name given it is, 'One World Trade Center.' For this reason, New York *could be*, not saying it will be the headquarters of Commercial Babylon.

## CHAPTER 13

# The Religious Harlot Destruction

*The human body is the 1st Wonder of the world because the human eyes are the only way we see the 7 Wonders of the world!*

– Chaplain Zachary

Don't worry scoffers, the apostate church shall be judged too. One atheist scoffer is asking, 'Where is the Christian God during the Coronavirus'? One 'openly gay' Senator in New York was very upset that the Billy Graham Foundation, Samaritan Purse, setup tents to help take care of New Yorker's during this COVID-19 pandemic. He tweeted his frustration at a 'bigoted' Christian organization helping victims of the Coronavirus. Never mind the overrun hospitals…all he saw was a religious group who is opposed to the LGBTQ+ lifestyle. He does not seem smart enough to know that their (LBGTQ+) beef is with God whom they shall stand before when they die and cast into Hell. I know he'll compare himself to me as being more successful because he is a Senator, and that's ok. There would be something wrong if he did not get elected in a Democratic *liberal* state.

The Holy Bible is not liberal. It never has been and never shall be. It is conservative. It teaches the Holiness of God. Therefore, it never has never been nor ever will support liberal views. There should no such thing as a liberal Christian. Those that identify as liberal deceives themselves Christians in fellowship with God.

"_12Behold, I come quickly; and my reward is with me, to render to each man according as his work is. 13I am the Alpha and the Omega, the first and the last, the beginning and the end. 14Blessed are they that wash their robes, that they may have the right to come to the tree of life, and may enter in by the gates into the city. 15Without are the dogs, and the sorcerers, and the fornicators, and the murderers, and the idolaters, and every one that loveth and maketh a lie. 16I Jesus have sent mine angel to testify unto you these things for the churches. I am the root and the offspring of David, the bright, the morning star. 17And the Spirit and the bride say, Come. And he that heareth, let him say, Come. And he that is athirst, let him come: he that will, let him take the water of life freely._" (Revelation 22:12-17)

Jesus shall judge the Apostate church led by the False Prophet (shaping up to be a Catholic Pope). The current Pope, Pope Francis (Jorge Mario Bergoglio), seeks– and has obtained signatures–of many different religious groups and united them as a 'One World Religion.' I have the YouTube video. It began with Pope John Paul II, at an interreligious prayer for peace in Assai on October 27, 1986.[29] The United Religions if officially born and its Charter was signed in June 2000.[30] On February 16, 2016, world religions signed an agreement to unite unconditionally. It is the equivalent of the United Nations.[31]

Never mind that Jesus clearly states He came to cause a division:

*"34Think not that I came to send peace on the earth: I came not to send peace, but a sword. 35For I came to set a man at variance against his father, and the daughter against her mother, and the daughter in law against her mother in law: 36and a man's foes' shall be they of his own household. 37He that loveth father or mother more than me is not worthy of me; and he that loveth son or daughter more than me is not worthy of me. 38And he that doth not take his cross and follow after me, is not worthy of me. 39He that findeth his life shall lose it; and he that loseth his life for my sake shall find it."* (Matthew 10:34-39)

This division has eternal consequences. What the Pope initiated was a *compromise*, thus, opening the gates of hell wide open to receive deceived mankind. This apostasy was prophesied by the Apostle Paul in the book of 2nd Thessalonians and by Jesus when He addressed the spiritual condition of the Church of Laodicea:

---

[29] https://www.youtube.com/watch?v=foi-c2ElW6o
[30] http://www.baioministries.com/one-world-religion-now-officially-born.html
[31] https://www.youtube.com/watch?v=HTuds8DiHiE

"*1Now we beseech you, brethren, touching the coming of our Lord Jesus Christ, and our gathering together unto him; 2to the end that ye be not quickly shaken from your mind, nor yet be troubled, either by spirit, or by word, or by epistle as from us, as that the day of the Lord is just at hand; 3let no man beguile you in any wise: for it will not be, except the falling away come first, and the man of sin be revealed, the son of perdition, 4he that opposeth and exalteth himself against all that is called God or that is worshipped; so that he sitteth in the temple of God, setting himself forth as God. 5Remember ye not, that, when I was yet with you, I told you these things? 6And now ye know that which restraineth, to the end that he may be revealed in his own season. 7For the*

*mystery of lawlessness doth already work: only there is one that restraineth now, until he be taken out of the way. 8And then shall be revealed the lawless one, whom the Lord Jesus shall slay with the breath of his mouth, and bring to nought by the manifestation of his coming; 9even he , whose coming is according to the working of Satan with all power and signs and lying wonders, 10and with all deceit of unrighteousness for them that perish; because they received not the love of the truth, that they might be saved. 11And for this cause God sendeth them a working of error, that they should believe a lie: 12that they all might be judged who believed not the truth, but had pleasure in unrighteousness.*" (2 Thessalonians 2:1-12)

And from the mouth of Jesus Himself to the *luke-warm*, end-time church:

"*14And to the angel of the church in Laodicea write: These things saith the Amen, the faithful and true witness, the beginning of the creation of God: 15I know thy works, that thou art neither cold nor hot: I would thou wert cold or hot. 16So because thou art lukewarm, and neither hot nor cold, I will spew thee out of my mouth. 17Because thou sayest, I am rich, and have gotten riches, and have need of nothing; and knowest not that thou art the wretched one and miserable and poor and blind and naked: 18I counsel thee to buy of me gold refined by fire, that thou mayest become rich; and white garments, that thou mayest clothe thyself, and that the shame of thy nakedness be not made manifest; and eyesalve to anoint thine eyes, that thou mayest see. 19As many as I love, I reprove and chasten: be zealous therefore, and repent. 20Behold, I stand at the door and knock: if any man hear my voice and open the door, I will come in to him, and will sup with him, and he with me. 21He that overcometh, I will give to him to sit down with me in my throne, as I also overcame, and sat down with my Father in his throne. 22He that hath an ear, let him hear what the Spirit saith to the churches.*" (Revelation 3:14-22)

*Clearly,* the church of our Lord and Savior Jesus the Christ was established as a nation set apart for evangelizing the lost to Christ. Christianity is a nation of believer's in Jesus as the 'only' way to heaven. The twelve Apostles are the foundation of the Christian faith. Twelve is the number for government in the Holy Bible. Jesus trained them and commissioned them to turn the world *right-side-up.* All religions do not serve the same God. What point would it be for the Holy Father to send Jesus to die on the cross if there were many religious routes to heaven? The United Religion is simply Satan doing what he does best…deceive!

Jesus made this very clear when He asked the Holy Father if there was any other way mankind could be saved:

*"36Then cometh Jesus with them unto a place called Gethsemane, and saith unto his disciples, Sit ye here, while I go yonder and pray. 37And he took with him Peter and the two sons of Zebedee, and began to be sorrowful and sore troubled. 38Then saith he unto them, My soul is exceeding sorrowful, even unto death: abide ye here, and watch with me. 39And he went forward a little, and fell on his face, and prayed, saying, My Father, if it be possible, let this cup pass away from me: nevertheless, not as I*

*will, but as thou wilt. 40And he cometh unto the disciples, and findeth them sleeping, and saith unto Peter, What, could ye not watch with me one hour? 41Watch and pray, that ye enter not into temptation: the spirit indeed is willing, but the flesh is weak. 42Again a second time he went away, and prayed, saying, My Father, if this cannot pass away, except I drink it, thy will be done. 43And he came again and found them sleeping, for their eyes were heavy. 44And he left them again, and went away, and prayed a third time, saying again the same words. 45Then cometh he to the disciples, and saith unto them, Sleep on now, and take your rest: behold, the hour is at hand, and the Son of man is betrayed into the hands of sinners. 46Arise, let us be going: behold, he is at hand that betrayeth me." (Matthew 26:36-46)*

God the Father, God the Son, and God the Holy Spirit is a witness against mankind that there was no other way for mankind to be saved. So then, why if the Pope uniting religions? Clearly, he is fulfilling prophecy He knows what the scriptures teach, and yet he has united all of the major religions under one umbrella, the United Religions.

So, for you scoffers, enjoy your scoffing, God is not mocked. All religions does lead to God...to be judged! Every Christ rejecting man and woman shall stand before Jesus and give an account. Jesus said that every idle word spoken shall man give an account:

*"36And I say unto you, that every idle word that men shall speak, they shall give account thereof in the day of judgment. 37For by thy words thou shalt be justified, and by thy words thou shalt be condemned." (Matthew 12:36-37)*

I am not giving these scriptures for my benefit...I'm saved. I am giving them in hope that those who may be reading this book and have never been taught the scriptures will know their final destination–Heaven of Hell, if they do not exercise a 'mustard seed' of faith! I encourage anyone wondering if Jesus is the real deal to simply pray: Dear LORD God, creator of heaven and earth, with all the religions in the world, please, reveal yourself to me that I may be saved. There is only one

God who created the heavens and the earth, and it is He who will hear and answer your prayer. Write down the day you prayed this prayer and the day He answered. Keep praying until you get an answer because your answer could be held up by Satan and his demonic spirits which is clearly taught in the book of Daniel, Chapter 10:

*"1In the third year of Cyrus king of Persia a thing was revealed unto Daniel, whose name was called Belteshazzar; and the thing was true, but the time appointed was long: and he understood the thing, and had understanding of the vision. 2In those days I Daniel was mourning three full weeks. 3I ate no pleasant bread, neither came flesh nor wine in my mouth, neither did I anoint myself at all, till three whole weeks were fulfilled. 4And in the four and twentieth day of the first month, as I was by the side of the great river, which is Hiddekel; 5Then I lifted up mine eyes, and looked, and behold a certain man clothed in linen, whose loins were girded with fine gold of Uphaz: 6His body also was like the beryl, and his face as the appearance of lightning, and his eyes as lamps of fire, and his arms and his feet like in colour to polished brass, and the voice of his words like the voice of a multitude. 7And I Daniel alone saw the vision: for the men that were with me saw not the vision; but a great quaking fell upon them, so that they fled to hide themselves. 8Therefore I was left alone, and saw this great vision, and there remained no strength in me: for my comeliness was turned in me into corruption, and I retained no strength. 9Yet heard I the voice of his words: and when I heard the voice of his words, then was I in a*

*deep sleep on my face, and my face toward the ground. 10And, behold, an hand touched me, which set me upon my knees and upon the palms of my hands. 11And he said unto me, O Daniel, a man greatly beloved, understand the words that I speak unto thee, and stand upright: for unto thee am I now sent. And when he had spoken this word unto me, I stood trembling. 12Then said he unto me, Fear not, Daniel: for from the first day that thou didst set thine heart to understand, and to chasten thyself before thy God, thy words were heard, and I am come for thy words. 13But the prince of the kingdom of Persia withstood me one and twenty days: but, lo, Michael, one of the chief princes, came to help me; and I remained there with the kings of Persia. 14Now I am come to make thee understand what shall befall thy people in the latter days: for yet the vision is for many days." (Daniel 10:1-14, KJV).*

Verse 10-14 clearly states that the angel Gabriel was detained by Satan and his demonic angels for 21 days. So, don't stop praying until you get your answer.

No other book ever written gives an insight into heaven but the Holy Bible. You may have been deceived into believing that the Holy Scripture were written by men and changed over the years. That is a lie of the devil! Holy men wrote as they were moved by the Holy Spirit (2 Peter 1:16-21). Here is an insight into heaven and those who died in faith in Jesus the Christ:

"<u>9</u>I beheld till thrones were placed, and one that was ancient of days did sit: his raiment was white as snow, and the hair of his head like pure wool; his throne was fiery flames, and the wheels thereof burning fire. <u>10</u>A fiery stream issued and came forth from before him: thousands of thousands ministered unto him, and ten thousand times ten thousand stood before him: the judgment was set, and the books were opened." (Daniel 7:9-10)

And,

"<u>1</u>And I saw an angel coming down out of heaven, having the key of the abyss and a great chain in his hand. <u>2</u>And he laid hold on the dragon, the old serpent, which is the Devil and Satan, and bound him for a thousand years, <u>3</u>and cast him into the abyss, and shut it , and sealed it over him, that he should deceive the nations no more, until the thousand years should be finished: after this he must be loosed for a little time. <u>4</u>And I saw thrones, and they sat upon them, and judgment was given unto them: and I saw the souls of them that had been beheaded for the testimony of Jesus, and for the word of God, and such as worshipped not the beast, neither his image, and received not the mark upon their forehead and upon their hand; and they lived, and reigned with Christ a thousand years. <u>5</u>The rest of the dead lived not until the thousand years should be finished. This is the first resurrection. <u>6</u>Blessed and holy is he that hath part in the first resurrection: over these the second death hath no power; but they shall be priests of God and of Christ, and shall reign with him a thousand years." (Revelation 20:1-6)

No other book on the face of this earth gives these details about heaven. God gave them to His Prophets and Apostles to give to those who would exercise a *mustard seed* of faith (faith the size of a mustard seed) to be saved. The Apostle Paul would not describe his visit to heaven. He said words would not do heaven justice (2 Corinthians 12:1-5). So, for the scoffers…scoff on. I know who gets the last laugh.

## CHAPTER 14

# The New World Order

*There is a multitude of atheists and all other Christ rejectors who
believe Jesus is the Son of God, born of a Virgin, and died on the
cross for the sins of the world. Problem is, their witness of this truth
is while they are burning in Hell!*

– Chaplain Zachary

The world shall continue to degrade or *devolve* into a godless
society as the scriptures declare:

*"7And behold, I come quickly. Blessed is he that keepeth the
words of the prophecy of this book. 8And I John am he that heard and
saw these things. And when I heard and saw, I fell down to worship
before the feet of the angel that showed me these things. 9And he
saith unto me, See thou do it not: I am a fellow-servant with thee and
with thy brethren the prophets, and with them that keep the words of
this book: worship God. 10And he saith unto me, Seal not up the
words of the prophecy of this book; for the time is at hand. 11He that
is unrighteous, let him do unrighteousness still: and he that is filthy,
let him be made filthy still: and he that is righteous, let him do*

109

*righteousness still: and he that is holy, let him be made holy still."*
*(Rev 22:7-11)*

The book of Revelation tells us just how far away from God and the Holy Scriptures mankind shall fall leading up to the last seven years of human history.

## The Two Witnesses

*"1And there was given me a reed like unto a rod: and one said, Rise, and measure the temple of God, and the altar, and them that worship therein. 2And the court which is without the temple leave without, and measure it not; for it hath been given unto the nations: and the holy city shall they tread under foot forty and two months. 3And I will give unto my two witnesses, and they shall prophesy a thousand two hundred and threescore days, clothed in sackcloth. 4These are the two olive trees and the two candlesticks, standing before the Lord of the earth. 5And if any man desireth to hurt them, fire proceedeth out of their mouth and devoureth their enemies; and if any man shall desire to hurt them, in this manner must he be killed. 6These have the power to shut the heaven, that it rain not during the days of their prophecy: and they have power over the waters to turn them into blood, and to smite the earth with every plague, as often as they shall desire." (Rev 11:1-6)*

## The Witnesses Killed

*"7And when they shall have finished their testimony, the beast that cometh up out of the abyss shall make war with them, and*

*overcome them, and kill them. 8And their dead bodies lie in the street of the great city, which spiritually is called Sodom and Egypt, where also their Lord was crucified. 9And from among the peoples and tribes and tongues and nations do men look upon their dead bodies three days and a half, and suffer not their dead bodies to be laid in a tomb. 10And they that dwell on the earth rejoice over them, and make merry; and they shall send gifts one to another; because these two prophets tormented them that dwell on the earth." (Rev 11:7-10)*

**The Witnesses Resurrected**

*"11And after the three days and a half the breath of life from God entered into them, and they stood upon their feet; and great fear fell upon them that beheld them. 12And they heard a great voice from heaven saying unto them, Come up hither. And they went up into heaven in the cloud; and their enemies beheld them. 13And in that hour there was a great earthquake, and the tenth part of the city fell; and there were killed in the earthquake seven thousand persons: and the rest were affrighted, and gave glory to the God of heaven. 14The second Woe is past: behold, the third Woe cometh quickly." (Rev 11:11-14)*

We see how people will celebrate God's Prophets sent to turn the hearts of the people to God. The problem is, they do not want God ruling over their lives. A Black man walked up to a police car in Los Angeles, CA and shot them and people were outside the hospital shouting they hope they die! God's standards are too conservative, too restrictive. Notice the

111

definite time period they will witness for God…3 ½ years. It is God who allows them to be killed and we see great rejoicing by godless people. They send gifts to one another as they see the two men promoting the conservative values of God. Mankind doesn't want their sins addressed. Mankind has always sought a 'feel good' social environment…if it feels good–*do it!*

Herod Antipas took his brother's wife from him and John the Baptist spoke out against it and his wife had John beheaded while he was in prison:

"*1At that season Herod the tetrarch heard the report concerning Jesus, 2and said unto his servants, This is John the Baptist; he is risen from the dead; and therefore do these powers work in him. 3For Herod had laid hold on John, and bound him, and put him in prison for the sake of Herodias, his brother Philip's wife. 4For John said unto him, It is not lawful for thee to have her. 5And when he would have put him to death, he feared the multitude, because they counted him as a prophet. 6But when Herod's birthday came, the daughter of Herodias danced in the midst, and pleased Herod. 7Whereupon he promised with an oath to give her whatsoever she should ask. 8And she, being put forward by her mother, saith, Give me here on a platter the head of John the Baptist. 9And the king was grieved; but for the sake of his oaths, and of them that sat at meat with him, he commanded it to be given; 10and he sent and beheaded John in the prison. 11And his head was brought on a platter, and given to the damsel: and she brought it to her mother. 12And his disciples came, and took up the corpse, and buried him; and they went and told Jesus." (Matthew 14:1-12)*

This is the prevalent attitude that shall dominate a godless society in the last days. A society having no fear of God. A 'cancel' and a 'woke' culture. During this COVID-19 Pandemic, abortion clinics were deemed essential and needed to stay open while churches were closed. This shows that we are not far from a completely godless society in 2020.

## Preparation for a New World Order

Before the 2nd Coming of Jesus, the whole world will be all shook up a *second* time!

*"17And the seventh poured out his bowl upon the air; and there came forth a great voice out of the temple, from the throne, saying, It is done: 18and there were lightnings, and voices, and thunders; and there was a great earthquake, such as was not since there were men upon the earth, so great an earthquake, so mighty. 19And the great city was divided into three parts, and the cities of the nations fell: and Babylon the great was remembered in the sight of God, to give unto her the cup of the wine of the fierceness of his wrath. 20And every island fled away, and the mountains were not found. 21And great hail, every stone about the weight of a talent, cometh down out of heaven upon men: and men blasphemed God because of the plague of the hail; for the plague thereof is exceeding great." (Rev 16:17-21)*

At this earthquake there will be no more cell phone towers, no airport towers, no gas stations (they will explode), no telephone poles, no television, no factories (car, clothing, etc.), no banks, no computer communications (landline or wireless), no grocery stores, no smartphones, and the list goes on. In that earthquake, it will change back to the days after the flood when men gathered lives stock and farmed the land. Back in the days of Adam and Eve and after the flood in the days of Noah, Job, and Abraham. A man might find a tractor with gas in it and it might start, but how would he get a new battery or more gas or repair parts...*he won't*. Everyone would be financially equal...*broke*; and will need to find shelter, food, and water. What is sheltering in a house with no food or water? Many will just commit suicide, as many did during the Great Depression.

At the 2$^{nd}$ Coming of Jesus will be a new world order.

Transportation will be foot, cart, horses, and beasts of burden. The Green New Deal touted by progressive Democrats will be in full effect after the judgments that are poured out on the earth during the 3 1/2 year Great Tribulation, except Jesus will be ruling in righteousness as King of the whole earth. There will be an equal distribution of wealth. Childbirth will be natural, and all women will breastfeed. No pampers, just cloth diapers. No washing machine but buckets of water by a river. No prescription pills, but herbs. No instant news of events happening around the world, but news carriers on horseback. No territorial disputes, no wars for the book of Zechariah declares that Jesus will hold back the rain and lives will begin to die as in a famine. First livestock, then people, as was the seven years of plenty followed by the seven years of famine mentioned in the book of Genesis under Joseph's leadership. In addition, Jesus will send plagues (virus):

*"16And it shall come to pass, that every one that is left of all the nations that came against Jerusalem shall go up from year to year to worship the King, Jehovah of hosts, and to keep the feast of tabernacles. 17And it shall be, that whoso of all the families of the earth goeth not up unto Jerusalem to worship the King, Jehovah of hosts, upon them there shall be no rain. 18And if the family of Egypt go not up, and come not, neither'shall it be upon them; there shall be the plague wherewith Jehovah will smite the nations that go not up to keep the feast of tabernacles. 19This shall be the punishment of Egypt, and the punishment of all the nations that go not up to keep the feast of tabernacles. 20In that day shall there be upon the bells of the horses, HOLY UNTO JEHOVAH; and the pots in Jehovah's house shall be like the bowls before the altar. 21Yea, every pot in Jerusalem and in Judah shall be holy unto Jehovah of hosts; and all they that sacrifice shall come and take of them, and boil therein: and in that day there shall be no more a Canaanite in the house of Jehovah of hosts."* (Zechariah 14:16-21)

## CHAPTER 15

# Time Is at Hand

I want to share the latest *Christian* timeline with permission by Prophecy Watcher, Diamond Duck. This timeline is for those very familiar with their Bible:[32]

Time is At Hand

"At Hand - By Daymond Duck - May 24, 2020.

A reader recently e-mailed me Hal Lindsey's quote, "The coming of the Lord is at hand" (James 5:8).

This great prophecy teacher pointed out that "at hand" does not mean that the Rapture would happen in the next few years (although it could have).

"At hand" means the Rapture will happen at any time and without warning.

"At hand" is an admonition for everyone in every generation to be ready to go at any moment, all the time.

There is a lot of misunderstanding about this issue. God told Adam if he ate of the fruit of the tree of the knowledge of

---

[32] https://www.raptureready.com/2020/05/24/at-hand-by-daymond-duck/

good and evil, he would die in that day (Gen. 2:17). Adam ate the fruit, but he did not die within 24 hours; he died when he was 930 years old (Gen.5:5).

1,000 years in man's eyes are like one day to God (Psa. 90:4; II Pet. 3:8).

Some Christians believe that "last days" sometimes refers to days 5, 6 and 7 of a 7,000 year cycle (two 1,000-year God-days called the Church Age and one 1,000-year God-day called the Millennium (Heb. 1:1-2; I Pet. 1:20; James 5:3; II Pet. 3:3).

The first 4 God-days (4,000 years; equivalent to our Sun., Mon., Tue. and Wed.) ran from Adam to the first coming of Jesus.

The last 3 God-days (last 3,000 years; 2 days of Church Age and 1 day of rest called the Millennium; equivalent to our Thur., Fri. and Sat.) run from the first coming of Jesus to the end of the millennium.

Don't forget that Peter called the beginning of the Church on Pentecost the fulfillment of Joel's prophecy of the last days (Acts 2:16-18).

Days 5 and 6 (two 1,000-year God-days) began when the Holy Spirit was "poured out" on Pentecost (Acts 2:17), and they will end when the Holy Spirit is "taken out" of the way at the Rapture of the Church (II Thess. 2:7).

It is debatable, but according to Catholic tradition, Jesus was crucified and the Church began in 30 A.D. (others say 30-33 A.D.).

Now, take note of the fact that the UN goal of a world government by 2030 is exactly 2,000 years or two God-days from the possible beginning of the Church.

Below are more reasons to believe that the Church could be in the last hours of the Church Age (last hours of the last days on God's clock).

**One,** concerning tracking everyone, a new bill called the "Covid-19 Testing, Reaching, And Contacting Everyone (TRACE) Act has passed and been signed.

TRACE originated in the House of Representatives and, for some strange reason, it is numbered H.R. 6666.

H.R. 6666 appropriates $100 billion to trace and monitor people that have come in contact with someone that has (or has had) the Coronavirus, plus it hints at more money for future use (monitoring that could extend into the Tribulation Period).

Monitoring includes mobile testing stations; visiting people in their homes, if necessary; requiring (forcing) people to be tested for the Coronavirus; and "other purposes" (a phrase with ominous overtones).

119

This is more evidence that the Mark of the Beast prophecy is literal, and the Tribulation Period could be close.

**Two,** in mid-May 2020, the Mayor of Los Angeles, Cal., said he

intends to send city employees and volunteers to visit defiant businesses that are open and urge them to voluntarily close.

People that refuse to voluntarily close will have their water and electricity shut off (city will not sell, and businesses will not be allowed to buy water and electricity).

FYI: For more details on these first two items, listen to the message by J.D. Farag at this link: https://www.youtube.com/watch?v=RPvghpK3oxk

**Three,** on May 12, 2020, the Director of the National Institute of Allergy and Infectious Diseases (NIAID), Dr. Anthony Fauci, was addressing a U.S. Senate Committee about the development of a vaccine for the coronavirus when he said he is cautiously optimistic, but "There's no guarantee that the vaccine is actually going to be effective." Pray that an effective vaccine will be found but know that man cannot do anything without God's permission, and make sure you are saved in case He does not grant it.

**Four,** on May 11, 2020, Israel announced that Israel's Health Ministry will immediately start offering voluntary blood tests at existing clinics.

Israel's health officials believe some people may have been exposed to the virus and developed an immunity to it. These officials plan to test 100,000 volunteers for antibodies that show an immunity. If some people are immune to the virus, they do not need to be vaccinated or quarantined; they can go back to work, travel, etc. If this is true, a law requiring everyone on earth to be vaccinated and tattooed may be unnecessary.

**Five,** on May 15, 2020, Executives at Sorrento Therapeutics in California said they have discovered a Coronavirus antibody that has been 100% effective in lab tests. They said the antibody will protect healthy cells from the virus and get rid of it in 4 days.

**Six,** concerning world religion and his departing from the faith, on May 10, 2020, possible (emphasis on possible) False Prophet, Pope Francis said, "I believe that should he (Trump) be re-elected,

God will abandon all of his blessings upon America, and may see fit to raze it down, as Sodom and Gomorrah."

Pope Francis should know that the problem in Sodom and Gomorrah was homosexuality, not people like Trump (Gen.

19:1-28). Pope Francis has departed from the traditional Roman Catholic teaching (and the teaching of Pope Benedict) that homosexuality is unchristian.

Concerning America's future, Anne Graham Lotz (Billy Graham's daughter) said it well, "For years we've (American's have) been telling God to get out of our schools, to get out of our government and to get out of our lives. And being the Gentleman

He is, I believe He has calmly backed out. How can we expect God to give us His blessing and His protection if we demand He leave us alone?"

**Seven,** on May 14, 2020, U.S. Sec. of State Mike Pompeo was in

Israel to: 1) try to advance Pres. Trump's Peace to Prosperity proposal, and 2) to discuss the Israeli annexation of parts of Judea and Samaria.

These two issues relate to prophecies that must happen *after* the Rapture.

The Antichrist must confirm a covenant of peace before the Tribulation Period can begin (Dan. 9:27; there could be swift movement after the rapture of the Church, plus many Arabs are beginning to move away from the Palestinians and toward Israel).

The Palestinians want all Jews out of Judea and Samaria, but Jesus revealed that there will be a Temple, and Jews living in Judea at the middle of the Tribulation Period (Matt. 24:15-16).

In exchange for Israel's written assurance that Israel will make an honest effort to negotiate a final peace treaty with the Palestinians, the U.S. is ready to recognize Israel's annexation of about 30% of Judea and Samaria (There has been some wavering in Israel because of threats from the UN, EU, Palestinians, Jordan and others, but at this time it looks like Israel plans to vote on it around July 1, 2020).

Advancing Trump's peace proposal and annexing 30% of Judea and Samaria does not mean that the Tribulation Period is close (the Ten Kings haven't appeared, Elijah hasn't appeared, etc.), but it seems evident that the Tribulation Period is shaping up, and dividing Israel has ominous implications for the Battle of Armageddon (Joel 3:2).

Prime Min. Netanyahu said, "I think that this (Israel's new government) is an opportunity to promote peace and security (peace and safety), based on the understandings that I reached with President Trump (during) my last visit in Washington in January."

The promotion of peace and safety is a major sign that the Tribulation Period could be close (I Thess. 5:3), and Trump's peace proposal is like fuel on a fire. The creation of a map by

Israel and the U.S. that will divide the Promised Land (if agreed to) and set aside 70% of Judea and Samaria for a potential Palestinian State, the freezing of Israeli construction on 70% of Judea and Samaria for four years, and the abandonment of 10,000 Jews to Palestinian control transgress the warnings of God.

Finally, there is always hope for every individual and nation.

God is all-powerful, God can destroy, God can deliver, and God offers hope to individuals and nations that do not know Him or that have abandoned Him (Jer. 1:10; II Chron. 7:14).

But the Bible is very clear that truly accepting Jesus as one's Lord and Savior is the only way to be saved (John 14:6; Acts

4:12), and the Rapture is the only hope of the terminal generation (Titus 2:13).

Be sure that you are trusting in Jesus and nothing else, draw close to Him, repent of your sins, and no matter what happens you will come out on top (Joel 2:11-13)."

Because the Rapture is at hand, the time to act is now.

Prophecy Plus Ministries, Inc.

Daymond & Rachel Duck

duck_daymond@yahoo.com"

Remarkable

Below is another fascinating article by Daymond Duck I thought was very relevant for us as Christians and especially we as Bible Prophecy watchers:[33]

"This article begins with a list of remarkable facts that some readers already know.

The Jewish Talmud, Barnabus (a companion of Paul), Irenaeus, Justin Martyr and others taught that the earth would go through a 7,000-year cycle (6,000 years of human rule and 1,000 years of

Messiah's rule), and the last days of man's 6,000 years are about up (1,000 years of our time is like one day to God; The last days of human rule started almost 2,000 years ago (Gen.2:17, 5:5; II Pet. 3:8; Acts 2:17).

Psalm 90 is called a prayer of Moses, and not all agree, but many believe that verse 10 teaches that a generation is 70-80 years. (Only God knows, but we could be the terminal generation that Jesus talked about in Matt. 24:34.)

The word "Trump" appears twice in the Bible, and both passages are about the Rapture (I Cor. 15:52; I Thess. 4:16).

Trump was born 700 days before Israel became a nation in 1948; he won the election by a margin of 77 votes; and he was

---

[33] https://www.raptureready.com/2020/05/03/remarkable-by-daymond-duck/

70 years, 7 months, and 7 days old on the day he was inaugurated.

Prime Min. Netanyahu had been in office 7 years, 7 months, and 7 days on the day that Donald Trump was elected.

Trump recognized Israeli sovereignty over the Golan Heights in Israel's 70th year.

Trump moved the U.S. Embassy to Jerusalem on Israel's 70th birthday.

Trump's Sec. of State, Mike Pompeo, is the 70th person to hold the job, and he accepted it in Israel's 70th year of existence.

On Apr. 14, 2020, the world population meter hit 7,777,777,777

(10-7's), and prophetically speaking, 10 is usually considered to be the number of completeness.

On Mar. 26, 2020, Microsoft published its application (filed internationally on 6-20-2019 under the number WO2020060606, which means World Order 2020 666) for a patent on a Cryptocurrency System Using Body Activity Data (technology that will connect a person to a computer over a cell phone, or whatever, and allow that person to scan a tattoo or a Mark that will grant access to a Cryptocurrency that can be tracked and used to buy and sell).

Microsoft's patent, World Order 2020 060606, is not the Mark of the Beast yet; it is not mandatory yet; the False Prophet is not involved yet, but an international patent on a system to track buying and selling that is numbered 666 (the number of the Antichrist's name; Rev. 13:18) could be a sign that the Mark of the Beast System is being developed.

By the way, the word "Mark" is where we get our word "tattoo."

The Mark of the Beast will be in a person's right hand or in their forehead, and Gates wants to put the tattoo under a person's skin.

This list has been compiled because the 6,000 years of human rule, a possible terminal generation of 70-80 years, a President named Trump, the unusual appearance of the number 7, and the World

Order number 060606 on a patent application to track buying and selling have converged in this generation.

The significance may be questionable, but the facts are remarkable, and there is the possibility that God could be using these facts to alert those that are watching.

Consider this:

In less than three months, the global economy has almost been destroyed;

several oil companies are facing bankruptcy;

millions of jobs have been lost;

the U.S. Constitution has been trampled upon; several institutions (churches, schools, colleges, etc.) have been disrupted;

Christians have been told not to go to Church, not to shake hands, not to hug;

more than 200,000 people have died;

thousands of families didn't get to say goodbye and many did not get to provide a normal funeral;

supply chains have been disrupted;

there have been some cases of panic buying; some store shelves have empty spaces;

some in the military have the virus;

some hospitals have been overrun;

many businesses have closed (some permanently);

drones from China are watching people in Connecticut to see if they are social distancing, coughing or sneezing;

Pope Francis is pushing a world government, a world religion, wealth redistribution, and more.

Yes, there are people that make themselves willingly ignorant of what is going on, but there are also many excellent prophecy teachers who understand that Jesus indicated there will be a convergence of the signs at the end of the age, and they realize that at least some of this relates to Bible prophecy.

Many believe Bible prophecy is being fulfilled all around us and we are getting just a tiny glimpse of what the Tribulation Period will be like.

Here are some more remarkable facts.

**One,** on Apr. 20, 2020, Benjamin Netanyahu and Benny Gantz agreed to form a new National Emergency Unity Government.

On July 1, 2020, they will initiate legislation to annex several areas in the West Bank (Judea and Samaria).

Expanding Israel's borders is a good thing, but there is a big problem.

Israel and the U.S. are proposing a map that will divide Israel and set aside perhaps as much as 2/3 of Judea and Samaria for a Palestinian state.

The good news is that the Palestinians probably will not accept that; but more importantly, God will not accept it either, and He may respond (see Joel 3:2).

**Two,** on Apr. 21, 2020, it was reported that YouTube CEO Susan Wojcicki admitted that YouTube has removed thousands of videos because they contradict World Health Organization (WHO) recommendations.

So, the Director-General of the WHO is a Communist from Ethiopia; his main support comes from China; Pres. Trump has suspended U.S. contributions to the WHO for parroting China's lies and mishandling the Coronavirus Crisis; the U.S. States of Missouri and Mississippi are suing China for lying; and YouTube is censoring those that contradict what the liars at the WHO say.

Truth and freedom will not be tolerated in the coming world government; and lest we forget, the WHO is working with Bill Gates, Dr. Fauci and George Soros to force everyone on earth to be vaccinated and tattooed (Marked), if they want to work, buy and sell.

**Three,** on Apr. 22, 2020, it was reported that 19 members of the G-20 held a virtual meeting and called for a document to be signed to strengthen the WHO and put it in charge of a coordinated worldwide response to the Coronavirus Crisis.

Trump did not participate, but if he had not blocked it, the WHO would have already been empowered to mark and track everyone on earth (see Rev. 13:15-17).

Considering what the U.S. Constitution says, why should U.S. citizens be forced to obey an unelected organization (the WHO) composed mostly of foreigners under a lying Communist leader that is influenced by Gates, Soros and Fauci?

**Four,** on Apr. 21, 2020, the Executive Director of the World Food Programme told the UN Security Council the Coronavirus Crisis may cause widespread famine of Biblical proportions in more than 30 African nations (see Rev. 6:5-8).

We are now being told that there is a chance of some food shortages in the U.S.

**Five,** on Apr. 24, 2020, UN Sec. Gen. Guterres announced that the Global Vaccination Response Team will be headed up by French Pres. Emmanuel Macron and Melinda Gates.

Macron is an avid supporter of the New World Order, and Gates is the wife of Bill Gates, a strong advocate for population control, mandatory vaccinations and digital tracking of everyone on earth.

It is impossible to overemphasize how remarkable and dangerous these events are.

The globalists are not going to wait until Jan. 1, 2030 and try to get a one-world government up and running in one day.

Laws must be written and put into practice; many groups, including the 10 Kings, must be approved, staffed and funded;

offices and equipment must be acquired; those that oppose it must be brought under control; a global economic system must be established; the world government must be funded (Guterres recently asked for a 10% global tax), and more.

The process of bringing this about appears to have started, the globalists are not going to back off, they are going to become more aggressive, and where the Bible says this is going is more dangerous than the Coronavirus.

Right now, they are trying to put America's healthcare system under the control of the WHO, shutting the doors of America's churches to bring Christianity under control, seeking to replace America's currency with a digital system, initiating a surveillance system tied to a global ID to track everyone on earth, and this is just the beginning.

The Rapture is probably close, but if there is a little more time, there is no telling what the globalists will do (or what God will do) as the world moves closer to 2030 and the globalist desire for a world government and a global ethic.

The certainty of our salvation and the need to get the gospel out are urgent matters.

The Tribulation period will be the greatest disaster to ever come upon Planet Earth (Matt. 24:21-22; Matt. 24:5-7).

Do not be deceived: if God has decided that it is time to let the globalists have their world government, it is coming, and nothing short of a major revival will slow it down.

Some think a major revival is coming, but I believe the Church will be lukewarm at the end-of-the-age, and the multitude of salvations they are referring to will be in the Tribulation Period (144,000 children of Israel, Two Witnesses and angel).

The Christian's hope is the Rapture of the Church (Titus 2:13), not the UN, national leaders, vaccinations, tracking systems, social distancing, masks or anything like that.

The only thing that God will accept to let a person into heaven is to sincerely believe what the Bible says about the birth, death, burial and resurrection of Jesus (Acts 16:30-33), confess that belief, and ask Jesus for forgiveness and salvation.

The remarkable thing is that He will grant it, and it is free to those that sincerely ask.

Do it now."

Prophecy Plus Ministries, Inc.

Daymond & Rachel Duck

duck_daymond@yahoo.com

## CHAPTER 16

# 244 Years a Slave in America – Why Blacks?

*For the Christ rejecters still alive and kicking, scientists has proved there is a Creator because of the orderliness of the Earth and its rotation, and Mankind's ability to leave the earth…*

*something monkeys have yet to do!*

– Chaplain Zachary

This reflects *'my'* personal comfort of *'why'* Blacks?

244 years a Slave (1619-1863)

101 years of Segregation (1863-1964)

345 years of *hatred* towards the White man (1619-1964)

56 years and counting, MLK Jr., "…little white boys and little white girls *play together* with little black boys and little black girls…" (1964-2020)

September 11, 2001, stunned the world, but it was local to

America as Muslim terrorists tried to take down the 'great dragon' as they describe America. Every 400 years God judges a nation. He will allow a nation's enemy to be His instrument of judgement. We know this from the book of Genesis, this was spoken by God to Abraham.

"*12Now when the sun was going down, a deep sleep fell upon Abram; and behold, horror and great darkness fell upon him. 13Then He said to Abram: "Know certainly that your descendants will be strangers in a land that is not theirs, and will*

*serve them, and they will afflict them four hundred years. 14And also the nation whom they serve I will judge; afterward they shall come out with great possessions. 15Now as for you, you shall go to your fathers in peace; you shall be buried at a good old age. 16But in the fourth generation they shall return here, for the iniquity of the Amorites is not yet complete" (Genesis 15:12-16).*

It is here the 'Oracle' of God is very clear '400' is the number for judgment for a nation. I firmly believe 9/11 was the 400th year of judgment for America because her enemy came here to attack her. Just this year I have a peace where I never had in trying to understand why God allowed Africans to be slaves. Not just here in America where is recorded the worst of the inhumane treatment of a race of people, but in all the nations we were slaves. The peace I have came for the scriptures earlier this year (2020) as I shared with my Pastor, Pastor Charlie Flores, Calvary Chapel East, El Paso, TX. The peace came directly from God the Holy Spirit after I cried, deeply, after watching 'Freedom Road' staring Muhammad Ali. I blamed God because He allowed it. I know He had the power to stop it, but He let it go on for 241 years with 99 years of segregation following in its footsteps. I had searched the scriptures to tie African slavery to the Egyptians enslaving the Israelites for 400 years (actually 430 in total), but I could not connect the dots.

God said to Abraham that his descendants would be delivered and that He would judge the nation which He did with the ten plagues and drowned Pharaohs army in the Red Sea. That was the fulfilment of that portion of the covenant God made to Abraham. Even the judgment of Egypt in the book of Ezekiel, Chapters 29 thru 32, did not connect the dots for they are a 'base' nation to this day as God said:

"8Therefore thus saith the Lord Jehovah: Behold, I will bring a sword upon thee, and will cut off from thee man and beast. 9And the land of Egypt shall be a desolation and a waste; and they shall know that I am Jehovah. Because he hath said, The river is mine, and I have made it; 10therefore, behold, I am against thee, and against thy rivers, and I will make the land of Egypt an utter waste and desolation, from the tower of Seveneh even unto the border of Ethiopia. 11No foot of man shall pass through it, nor foot of beast shall pass through it, neither shall it be inhabited forty years." (Ezekiel 29:8-11).

As we can see, this was fulfilled and after 40 years, the judgment of Egypt was complete. The book of Joel speaks of a judgement of Egypt and Edom that was fulfilled as the last known Edomite was Herod, in the days of Jesus on the earth.

So then, why African slavery in the 17th Century? As stated, I could not tie it to a mistreatment of another nation in the scriptures, and it was made very clear to me by the Holy Spirit that Africa had come up for judgment before God. I do not know what transpired four hundred years before Africans were taken as slaves. I do not know what 'gods' they served or anything about their tribal wars or more importantly, what abominations they practiced. I am at peace knowing that God has no respect a nation and it was simply that their time for judgment had come. I believe this was the same fate of Native American who was here before the White man came. The end result is that I am a Christian, something that might not be had not Blacks embraced the gospel of Jesus during slavery in America.

In connection with God's pattern of judgment is 'deliverance.' When the nation of Israel was judged by God, he let their enemy come and take them out of the land and their wealth. After 20, 30, 40, and the last recorded 70-year judgment of Israel, God always raised up a 'deliverer.' The most famous of Israel's deliverers was Sampson. His strength was connected with his hair. At the end of the 70-year captivity of Israel in Babylon, God raised up a deliver named

Cyrus, who was prophesied in the book of Isaiah, Chapter 45, where he is actually called 'God's Anointed.'

As did Israel's enemies, Britain came in a plundered the wealth of Africa for many years until God raised up a deliver...Bishop Tutu and Nelson Mandela. In America, He raised up Abraham Lincoln and Martin Luther King Jr. Of course, there were many others involved, but these two are the ones with statures honoring them. Notice, no stature of Malcom X because he was a man of violence and of a religion, Islam, that is 'Anti-Christ.' I understand why the black man embraced Islam; to get as far away as possible from the 'blue-eyed' Jesus of the White man. However, in doing so, they departed from their only means of salvation in Jesus the Christ.

Islam offers 'No' guarantee of salvation unless one become a Jihadist. How terribly sad to be part of a religion where your good must outweigh your bad on judgement day. A friend of mine, a converted Muslim to Christianity, said the Hadith, which teach about the life of Muhammad and the Quran teach that 'Hell' is filled with more Muslim women than men. A Muslim man can have four wives if he can afford separate dwellings for them, but the woman can have only one husband at a time. So then, to live as a Muslim woman with the men foot on their necks about what they can and cannot do in public and privately, raise their children in the Muslim way, do all that is required of Muslim women, and still end up in 'Hell' when they die 'if' their good deeds doesn't outweigh their bad deeds is a 'damnable' religion.

Every religion in the world can see that their 'gods' have no power whatsoever! I really pray they take notice as Egypt did when the ten plagues were complete. One might want to include Jesus with the powerless 'gods' of the world, but they are confused as to the 'free-will' they have exercised, granted by God, to accept or reject mankind's only hope of salvation in Jesus the Christ. The Church, a body of believers in Jesus the Christ, is the 'restraining' force against evil in the world today. And we have God, the Holy Spirit, dwelling withing us that, come what may, we are sure of our salvation. Only in Christianity has God stated that He desires that none should perish, but that all would embrace the cross of Jesus that they might be saved. The Holy Spirit has interacted with us and we, know that we know, that He dwells within us through His convictions and our weeping over sins when fellowship with the Father is broken.

Only Christianity has *named* and *dealt* with the 'sin' issue of man at the cross of Jesus. Muslim's say, 'Allah forgives sins when a Muslim ask. There was no need for anyone to die on a cross for other people sins.' Well, if that's the case, why doesn't the Muslim have an assurance of salvation if their good doesn't outweigh their bad? It is because it is 'nonsense' the rhetoric that Islam teaches. Without the Holy Spirit, there would be no Christianity. In America, without the Holy Spirit indwelling the members of the Church, we would not come together and pray and hold candle vigils when tragedy strikes. The love of many would surely wax cold without the spirit of the 'born again' child of God interceding against the evils of this world.

"*43Ye have heard that it was said, Thou shalt love thy neighbor, and hate thine enemy: 44but I say unto you, love your enemies, and pray for them that persecute you; 45that ye may be sons of your Father who is in heaven: for he maketh his sun to rise on the evil and the good, and sendeth rain on the just and the unjust. 46For if ye love them that love you, what reward have ye? do not even the publicans the same? 47And if ye salute your brethren only, what do ye more than others? do not even the Gentiles the same? 48Ye therefore shall be perfect, as your heavenly Father is perfect.*" (Matthew 5:43-48)

This verse of scripture is radical in that it goes against the norm, and assuredly, without the Holy Spirit, it is not possible for a people that was enslaved to forgive those who enslaved them. The Church of our Lord and Savior Jesus the Christ is the 'salt,' the preserving agent in the world today through our prayers and fasting.

As with Israel, when they called out to God as a nation, as one voice, God intervened. This He also did for the African in America, as our fore parents called on Jesus. So, I am at peace with why African slavery took place around the world and especially here in America. Though this book is about the Coronavirus, I hope this insight on slavery in America can bring closure to many of my race.

As I see it now, Black slaves prayed to Jesus and the Father answered our prayers as Jesus said to ask the Father anything in His name and He will do it. Black slaves prayed and was eventually set free.

With segregation, the Reverend Doctor Martin Luther King Jr. led a peaceful march with the New Testament as his banner and the Father honored the Blacks with an end to segregation. God also honored Martin Luther King Jr. as he honored Evangelist Billy Graham. Who has not been honored by God is Malcom X; 1) he wasn't a Christian, and 2) he advocated violence. He only mentioned him in history classes.

This time, with all of the violence in Democrat run cities allowed to play out, Blacks have picked up weapons and doing the opposite of Blacks slaves who prayed they received justice and equality. This outcome will be very different without Blacks, as a nation, praying to God for true justice that lasts.

The looting of stores is a disgrace to all educated conservative Black Christians. It is a disgrace when Blacks partake in the rioting under the pretense of obtaining justice. Blacks lead in abortion, school dropout, community crimes (with Mexicans), and filling low income jobs. It is mostly the reliance on the government for handouts because of the dangerous communities they still live in and Black Pastors preaching watered down messages from the pulpit. So, taking up weapons, rioting and looting is going to end badly for the Black community. An example, but very different, is God sending Jonah to Nineveh to warn them that they have come up for judgment before God. They repent. Nineveh is spared for 120-150 years. Then, God sends the Prophet Nahum to deliver the same message as Jonah, but this time Nineveh doesn't repent and God destroys Nineveh. As a Black community, we must unite in prayer for the future generations of the African American race. If not, God has no respect a person nor ethnic group nor nation.

# Master List of URLs Listed

https://bdnews24.com/world/asia-pacific/2020/05/21/in-chinas-crisis-xi-sees-a-crucible-to-strengthen-his-rule

2      https://foreignpolicy.com/2020/05/05/china-coronavirus-chaos-playbook-stability/

3 https://warontherocks.com/2016/04/a-new-generation-of-unrestricted-warfare/

4 https://www.foxnews.com/tech/china-is-using-economic-espionage-and-theft-to-grab-us-technology.

5      https://www.foxnews.com/media/alex-berenson-coronavirus-wuhan-lab-china.

6 https://www.rfa.org/english/news/china/concerns-03302020150737.html.

7 https://www.oann.com/virologist-says-there-is-evidence-covid-19-was-man-made-in-wuhan/

8 https://www.foxnews.com/shows/justice-jeanine.

9https://www.foxnews.com/world/who-chief-tedros-questionable-past-coronavirus.

10 https://www.modernworkplacelearning.com/cild/mwl/about/

[11] http://toddhampson.com/id2020-agenda2030/

[12] https:// https://www.covidcreds.com/

[13]https://www.medicinenet.com/script/main/art.asp?articlekey=2089
14.

[14] https://www.cdc.gov/flu/about/burden/index.html.

[15] https://www.ncbi.nlm.nih.gov/books/NBK209710/

[16] https://www.dailymail.co.uk/news/article-6424407/Every-person-spawned-single-pair-adults-living-200-000-years-ago-scientists-claim.html

[17] https://www.livescience.com/38613-genetic-adam-and-eve-uncovered.html

[18] https://study.com/academy/lesson/comparing-elements-on-earth-to-those-in-the-human-body.html

[19] https://www.cdc.gov/vhf/ebola/about.html

[20] https://www.wired.com/2004/05/film-raises-ire-over-hiv-origins/

[21] https://www.youtube.com/watch?v=TPpoJGYlW54

[22] https://www.who.int/ith/diseases/sars/en/

[23] https://www.the-scientist.com/news-analysis/sars-escaped-beijing-lab-twice-50137.

[24] https://www.history.com/topics/middle-ages/pandemics-timeline

[25] http://abq.fm/blog/another-virus-with-the-potential-to-cause-a-pandemic-was-discovered-in-none-other-than-china/

[26] https://www.history.com/topics/middle-ages/black-death.

[27] https://islamqa.info/en/answers/21457/more-women-in-hell-than-men

[28] https://en.wikipedia.org/wiki/1960_Valdivia_earthquake.

[29]https://www.washingtonpost.com/blogs/blogpost/post/bohemian-grove-where-the-rich-and-powerful-go-to-misbehave/2011/06/15/AGPV1sVH_blog.html

[30] https://www.youtube.com/watch?v=foi-c2ElW6o

[31] http://www.baioministries.com/one-world-religion-now-officially-born.html

[32] https://www.youtube.com/watch?v=HTuds8DiHiE

[33]https://www.raptureready.com/2020/05/24/at-hand-by-daymond-duck/

[34] https://www.raptureready.com/2020/05/03/remarkable-by-daymond-duck/

# About the Author

A lot of this book is intertwined with my personal struggles with evil in America and the world. I know that Sin is front and center of all of mankind's problem…and Satan. This is my only voice to the world. As Christians, we have 1) a voice, 2) prayer, and 3) a vote. I grew up on welfare in the projects in Houston, TX, with my mother and four brothers. I joined the Army at age 17. In July of 1979, that ended poverty for me. Of course, I sent money home every month, but poverty for me had ended. I can only credit God and my grandmother Lillian's prayers for rescuing me from the streets of South Park, Houston, TX. I did not know it was the LORD who led

147

me into the Army until years later after I rededicated my life to Christ. I retired after 25 years of active duty service with combat service in Operation Desert Storm. My last assignment was a Battle Staff Instructor at the Sergeant's Major Academy, Fort Bliss, TX, during OIF/OEF. After retirement, I was a Sr. Curriculum Developer at the same Academy as a contractor with General Dynamics. As a civilian contractor, I also spent 14 months as a Sr. Property Specialist at FOB Shindand, Kandahar, Afghanistan, with the 4/401st AFSB (2012-2014). I currently reside in El Paso, TX. I have two beautiful daughters and six grandchildren. I am currently enrolled in the D.Min program at SAGU (Aug 2020).

# Bonus: Praying the Names of God with the Disciples Prayer

## THE DISCIPLES PRAYER w/ THE NAMES OF GOD

Our Father who art in heaven, blessed dear Lord God, Blessed, Hollowed, Holy, and Awesome be Thy names, the names of Thy Son, Lord Jesus, and the names of Thy Holy Spirit:

Thy names, O, God, be **ELOHIM**, the creator and sustainer of all life from everlasting to everlasting, from eternity to eternity *(Genesis 1:1; John 1:1)!* Blessed be the agent of thy creation of this beautiful earth and the fulness therein, thy Son, Lord Jesus! Blessed be thy revelation to the Apostle Paul that all things were created by Him and for Him and without Him was not anything made that is not...because He did not *(Col 1:16-17; Hebrews 1:1-2)!*

Blessed, O, God, be the Holy Spirits role in creation! Bless Thee, Holy Spirit, for 'Empowering and Sustaining' the Church to this very second in time! Every time we read the Holy Scriptures, You, O, God, confirms in our Spirit that this is the Word/Oracle of God, and that Jesus is who He say He is! Thus, O, God, the church can continue for another 2000 years if you Father so decides!

Blessed, O, God, be Your 'Restraining Power' over evil to this very day! Thus, the Church of our Lord and Savior 'Must Be' taken out in the Rapture because we'll just keep praying, and praying, and praying – and the Gates of Hell shall 'NOT' prevail

*(1 Thess 2:6-8; 1 Cor 15:50-55)!* Blessed, O, God, be Thy ministry in the Earth and in the Life of the Believer! Blessed be every Man, Woman, and Child who have accepted Christ Jesus as our Lord and Savior...Past, Present, and Future! Blessed, O, God, is every man, woman, and child who is obedient to the guiding, the leading, and the teachings of the Holy Spirit! Blessed, O, God, be Israel, through whom we have salvation in the 'Jewish' Jesus (John 4:22). Blessed, O, God, Blessed, Hollowed, Holy, Wonderful, and totally Awesome be thy name.

I bless your name, **EL SHADDAI**, the God almighty of blessings *(Gen 49:15-16).* Thou, Heavenly Father, are our God and Father who 'Nourishes and Supplies,' thou art all Bountiful and all Sufficient! Blessed dear Lord God, Blessed, Hollowed, Holy, Wonderful, and Awesome be thy name.

I bless your name **ADONAI,** my Lord and my Master *(Gen*

*15:1; Judges 6:14-16).* Thou art, JEHOVAH, the completely self-existing one, always present and revealed in Jesus the Christ who is the same, Yesterday, Today, and Forever. Blessed dear Lord God, Blessed, Hollowed, Holy, Wonderful, and Awesome be thy name.

I bless your name, **EL OLAM**, the God of the Everlasting

Covenant: (1) Blessed, O, God, be thy covenant with Noah and his sons, never to destroy the earth again with a flood, and the covenant sign of the rainbow. Blessed, O, God, be thy blessing upon his three sons, Japheth, Shem, and Ham, to be fruitful and multiply and replenish the earth *(Gen 9:1-17),* that which we see to this very day. (2) Blessed, O, God, be thy covenant with Abraham, the Father of Faith, of the Godly line of Shem, that thru him, all the nations of the earth shall be blessed *(Gen 12:3).*

(3) Blessed, O, God, be thy covenant with Isaac and his son Jacob, whose name thy changed to Israel. Blessed be the twelve sons of Jacob, the nation of Israel *(Jere 32:38-44).* Blessed, O, God, be the wives of the Patriarchs, Sarah, Rebekah, Leah, and Rachael. (4) Blessed, O, God, be thy covenant with King David, a covenant which was fulfilled in Jesus the Christ, King of the Jews, Son of the Virgin Mary. (5) Blessed, O, God, be thy covenant with we, the Body of Jesus the Christ, that all who call on the name of Jesus shall be saved *(Roman 10:8-13).* (6)

Blessed, O, God, is thy covenant with the Tribulation Saints, that a remnant of Israel shall be saved and all they who do not take the Mark of the Beast, nor his Number, nor his Name. (7) Blessed, O, God, is the Second Coming of thy Son Lord Jesus and the Marriage Supper of the Lamb. (8) Blessed, O, God, is the Kingdom of Darkness 'bound' during the Millennial Reign of Christ for those 1000 years, and (8) Blessed be the final resting place of the Kingdom of Darkness in the Lake of Fire (Rev 19:20; 20:10-15). Blessed dear Lord God, Blessed, Hollowed, Holy, Wonderful, and totally Awesome be thy name!

I bless your name. **YHWH/JHVH** (YAHWEH/JEHOVAH), the Great 'I AM'! Thou, O, God, told Moses and Aaron to tell and Pharaoh...the God of the Hebrews [Israel], sent thee! Thou, O, God, Always Was and always Shall Be, the same, Yesterday, Today, and Forever *(Ex 3:13-15; 5:1-3)*. Blessed dear Lord God, Blessed, Hollowed, Holy, Wonderful, and Awesome be thy name.

I bless your name, **EL GIBBOR/GIBHOR** *(H1368)*, the Mighty God! Israel and we, the body of Jesus the Christ, we bless You and thank You, that while we're trying to figure things out, You have

already worked it out *(Is 9:6-7)*. Blessed dear Lord God, Blessed, Hollowed, Holy, Wonderful, and Awesome be thy name.

I bless your name, **JEHOVAH JIREH**, the one who sees our

needs, Israel and we, the body of Jesus the Christ, and provides for them *(Gen 22:11-14)*. Blessed dear Lord God, Blessed, Hollowed, Holy, Wonderful, and Awesome be thy name.

I bless your name, JEHOVAH SABAOTH, the Lord of Hosts

*(1 Sam 1:3)*. The God of Israel and we, the body of Jesus the Christ! We bless you and thank You that the Battle is Yours and the victory is we Your people. Blessed be the words of King David, 'Thou, O, Lord, teaches my hands to war *(Ps 18:34)*. Thou. O, Lord, teaches us to war in this 'Physical' world against the Seed of the Serpent and in the 'Spiritual' world against the Kingdom of Darkness! Blessed dear Lord God, Blessed, Hollowed, Holy, Wonderful, and Awesome be thy name.

I bless your name **JEHOVAH M'KADDESH/MEKODDISHKEM**, the LORD our Sanctifier *(Lev 20:6-8)!* Israel and we, the body of Jesus the Christ, we bless You and thank You for setting us apart for Yourself by sending your only begotten Son, Christ Jesus, to die on the cross for the sins of the world! Blessed be every Man, Woman, and Child who have accepted Thee, Lord Jesus, as our Lord and Savior...Past, Present, and Future! Blessed dear Lord

God, Blessed, Hollowed, Holy, Wonderful, and totally Awesome be thy name.

I bless your name **JEHOVAH RAPHA**, our healer! Thou, O, God, makes bitter experiences sweet! Israel and we the body

of Jesus Christ, we bless You and thank You for sending the Word made flesh and dwelt among us. By His Virgin Birth, His Sinless life, the Stripes across His back *(Is 53:5),* and His shed blood on the Cross, You have forgiven all of our iniquities and healed All of our diseases (Emotional healing that we may be able to endure the physical)! May we never forget that these bodies are a reminder that earth is not our home. Blessed dear Lord God, Blessed, Hollowed, Holy, Wonderful, and Awesome be thy name.

I bless you name **JEHOVAH NISSI**, our Victory, our Banner, our Standard! Your Banner of us is Love! When the enemy shall pour in like a flood, Israel and we, the body of Jesus the Christ, we bless Thee and thank Thee, that Thou, O, God, will lift up a Standard against him [Satan]! Blessed be the words of Kind David: The LORD is my shepherd; I shall not want. 2He maketh me to lie down in green pastures: he leadeth me beside the still waters. 3He restoreth my soul: he leadeth me in the paths of righteousness for his name's sake. 4Yea, though I walk through the valley of the shadow of death, I will fear no evil: for thou art with me; thy rod and thy staff they comfort me. 5Thou preparest a table before me in the presence of mine enemies: thou anointest my head with oil; my cup runneth over. 6Surely goodness and mercy shall follow me all the days of my life: and I will dwell in the house of the LORD forever. Therefore, we shall not fear, nor dread, nor be terrified, as one who has no hope *(Ex 17:8-15)!* Blessed dear Lord God, Blessed, Hollowed, Holy, Wonderful, and Awesome be thy name.

I bless your name, **JEHOVAH SHALOM**, our Peace! Israel and we, the body of Jesus the Christ, we bless Thee and thank Thee, O, Lord, for a peace that surpasses 'All' understanding; a peace that garrisons and mounts guard over our hearts and mind in Christ

Jesus *(Judges 6:17-24).* Blessed be the words of comfort Lord Jesus spoke unto us, 'Peace I leave with you, 'My Peace' I give unto you: not as the world giveth, give I unto you *(Jn 14:27).* Blessed dear Lord God, Blessed, Hollowed, Holy, Wonderful, and totally Awesome be thy name.

I bless your name **JEHOVAH TSIDKENU,** our Righteousness! Thank You for becoming Sin for us Lord Jesus, that Israel and we, Your body of Believers. may become the righteousness of our Father in heaven through Your shed blood on the Cross – and 'ONLY' by Your shed blood on the Cross *(Jere 33:14-16; 2 Cor 5:16-21).* Blessed dear Lord God,

Blessed, Hollowed, Holy, Wonderful, and Awesome be thy name.

I bless your name, **JEHOVAH ROI/ROHI**, thou are our Shepherd, Lord Jesus, Israel and we, thy body of Believers. We bless You and thank You that You will 'NEVER' leave us nor forsake us; we shall not want for any 'good or beneficial' thing *(Ps 23)*. Blessed dear Lord God, Blessed, Hollowed, Holy, Wonderful, and Awesome be thy name.

I bless your name, **JEHOVAH SHAMMAH**, Israel and we, the body of Jesus the Christ. We take comfort by the Holy Spirit and the Holy Scriptures. Because of Your Promises and Your Faithfulness, from generation to generation, we shall nor fear, nor dread, nor be terrified...what can mankind do unto us *(Ezek 48:30-35; Jn 14:1-4)!* Blessed be thy words, Lord Jesus, 'Fear 'NOT' him [Satan & the Children of the Devil] who is able to destroy the body, but afterwards have no more power; but fear HIM, who has the power to destroy 'Both' Body and Soul in Hell *(Matt 10:27-31)!* Blessed dear Lord God, Blessed,

Hollowed, Holy, Wonderful, and tremendously Awesome be thy name.

I bless your name, **EL ELYON**, the 'Most High' God, and the First Cause of Everything *(Duet 26:16-19)!* True Israel and we, the body of Jesus the Christ, our Soul and our Spirit testifies, that Thou, O, God, are the True and Living God – Worthy of all the Glory, Honor, and Praise, Dominion,

Majesty, and Power! Above thee, O, God, there is NONE other! There was NONE before thee, and there shall be NONE after Thee! There is but 'ONE GOD' revealed in 'Three Persons,' Thee Father, who is Jehovah, Thy Son Lord Jesus, who is Jehovah, and Thy Holy Spirit, who is Jehovah! "Beneath" thee, O, God, is the 'Unholy Trinity' – Satan, the Anti-Christ, and the False Prophet – to include 'All' of the Fallen Angels, and Dead gods men have made after their own bellies; having Eyes that cannot see, Ears that cannot hear, a Mouth that cannot speak, Feet that cannot move, Hands that cannot hold (unless made in the hold position)...dead gods like their makers...under the unction of Demonic Spirit that they be worshipped...and the Seed of the Serpent – 'ALL" of whom, Thou has made LORD Jesus' Foot Stool (*Lev 17:1-7; Ps 110:1, 115:1-8)!* Blessed dear Lord God, Blessed, Hollowed, Holy, Wonderful, and totally Awesome be thy name.

Thy Kingdom come, Thy Will be done, on earth, as it is in

heaven. Give us this day, we pray thee, our daily bread, and forgive us our debts, as we forgive us our debtors (*Matt 6:12).* Please forgive us our trespasses (intentional sins), as we forgive

those who trespass against us (*Mk 11:25-26).* Lead us not into temptation, but deliver us from evil, for Thine is the Kingdom, and the Power, and the Glory, Thee, thy Son, and thy Holy Spirit, forever, and ever. Amen *(Matt 6:9-13)*.